S0-ARN-234

Tackling Drug Problems in Public Housing:
A Guide for Police

Tackling Drug Problems in Public Housing:

A Guide for Police

by

Deborah Lamm Weisel
Police Executive Research Forum

North East Multi-Regional
Training, Inc.
1 Smoke Tree Plaza, Suite 111
North Aurora, IL   60542

The opinions expressed in this monograph are those of the author, and not necessarily those of the members of the Police Executive Research Forum.

Copyright © 1990, Police Executive Research Forum
Library of Congress Catalog Number: 90-061334
ISBN 1-878734-19-9

CONTENTS

FOREWORD

The nation's police officers and housing personnel and residents of public housing communities share an important goal: to effectively battle drug problems and provide an environment in which families can live free from the violence and influence of drug dealers who prey on those in public housing.

During my time at HUD, one of my top priorities has been to take back the public housing complexes from the grasp of drug dealers and return them to law-abiding citizens — citizens anxious to build a safe place for their families to live. In pursuing this objective, I have implemented such bold initiatives as easing eviction of drug traffickers, supporting innovative strategies to battle drug problems, funding housing security staffs, empowering the community to determine its own destiny, and furthering the promising concept of resident management and ownership.

Despite these anti-drug initiatives, the public housing environment simply cannot be stabilized without help from local authorities. Only if police and others are familiar with housing policies and rules, with management practices, and legal and fiscal constraints that affect day-to-day operations will they be able to work effectively with housing staffs and residents and be prepared to take on the challenge of securing a drug-free public housing environment. **Tackling Drug Problems in Public Housing: A Guide for Police** helps to fill this vital information need.

This book vividly describes today's public housing environment, explains how public housing evolved, and uses that information to suggest realistic means for improving conditions. Just as housing personnel are often unaware of the constraints under which police operate, there is a need for police to learn more about the housing environment.

Although **Tackling Drug Problems** is written for the police practitioner, any housing worker interested in ridding his or her community of drug-related problems should read this report as an important first step in forging stronger relationships with local police. The book describes in detail a specific plan for developing a collaborative and productive plan of action, based on carefully analyzing community problems in public housing. This problem-solving approach espoused by the Police Executive Research Forum draws upon actual experience in a number of cities and has met with significant success.

The public's support for anti-drug programs has never been stronger. Drug dealers have brought addiction, sickness and violence into the homes of too many citizens, especially the homes of those in public housing. Clearly, the only redress for such a deeply entrenched problem is coordinated action — action by law enforcement, housing officials and residents, teamed with social services, treatment, recreation and employment providers, to name a few. This book provides a plan for what we can achieve together; that plan foreshadows the demise of the parasitic drug dealer and the return of public housing to the people.

Jack Kemp,
Secretary, U.S. Department of
Housing and Urban Development

PREFACE

This book is not about being black or a single mother or poor, although these demographic characteristics do describe many public housing residents. Instead, this book is about police working with groups of people who, for complex reasons, are particularly vulnerable to drug dealing activity in their communities.

The reality of the 1990s is that few public housing residents are untouched by drug problems. The residents may be drug abusers, or may be buyers or sellers of drugs. They may be willing or unwilling accomplices to the drug trade or they may be beneficiaries of benevolent drug dealers. They may look up to drug dealers as successful role models, or, more frequently, they may be fearful onlookers or innocent viewers of drug activity in their community. Any of these scenarios or a combination may be true for an individual or family in public housing.

The reality is also that public housing residents are often condemned for their role in drug activity. Their communities may be written off, as having problems too complex for police or other public agencies to tackle. Yet because public housing residents are so concentrated and share some similar problems, tackling drug problems in public housing in concert with other agencies can yield rewarding results to police. And, if in the process, these results bring about improved economic conditions, ease racial tensions, improve access to services, or fill other economic or social gaps in troubled public housing communities, so much the better. What is important is not to fault the people and not to write off the community. What is important is to tackle, analytically and with interagency cooperation, the persistent problems that have become endemic in some troubled public housing.

The purpose of this guide is to provide police with a blueprint for understanding the workings of their local public housing authorities. This understanding may enhance the relationship between police, public housing officials and residents so that joint efforts can be made to improve the welfare of the larger community by addressing persistent problems, particularly drug-related problems, in public housing.

It is not the intent of this book to suggest that all public housing consists of troubled, huge and sprawling complexes, generating high rates of crime and filled with lawless minority residents. Indeed, there is much public housing in the United States which serves as decent and safe housing for some of the nation's poor families and the elderly. It is likely, however, that police will want to direct their scarce law enforcement resources to focus on that public housing which is the worst within a city.

This book is organized to provide the reader background material of substance about the organization and operations of public housing. This background material constitutes the first half of the monograph. The latter half of the document develops a strategy for using the knowledge about public housing to help solve persistent drug-related problems.

The first chapter, the Introduction, describes the troubled environment in which police and public housing agencies must operate. This section also describes the relevance of this topic for law enforcement officials.

The second chapter, Housing the Poor: An Historical Perspective of Public Housing, offers a concise history of the evolution of public housing.

The third chapter, Public Housing — A Closer Look, provides an inside view of the administrative operations of housing agencies, including descriptions of the agencies' relationships not only with police but also with the U.S. Department of Housing and Urban Development, residents, and local governing bodies.

Chapter 4 describes the common ground shared by police, housing agencies and public housing residents. This chapter sets the stage for Chapter 5, which suggests a process for developing a collaborative relationship between each of these groups.

The final chapter, Police Strategies Vary for Drug Problems in Public Housing, offers a brief description of a number of conjoint police and housing efforts around the country to battle drug problems. A glossary to the book is included to provide a concise definition of specialized housing terms.

It is important to note that the regulatory climate of public housing, and patterns of illegal drug activity, are constantly changing. Because of current interest in this area, federal and local policies regarding public housing are subject to change. Thus, although every effort has been made to produce an accurate document, caution should be taken in accepting at face value the information contained in this document. Instead, when possible, verification of policies and procedures should be determined locally.

Although many examples in this book are drawn from major urban areas, large-scale public housing is the exception rather than the rule. There are many examples of successful police initiatives related to drug problems in public housing being implemented around the country. These are occurring in small towns and cities, as well as in large cities. And, although there are major differences between problems in large urban centers and those in smaller cities, many of the problems encountered and potential strategies that can be used are similar, albeit on a different scale.

Indeed, this guide is not intended to be a prescription to solve local drug problems. Because drug problems are local in their nature, solutions should be developed locally. This book is intended only as a guideline for police in developing responses to drug-related problems in public housing.

ACKNOWLEDGMENTS

The need for this book became apparent during work done by the Police Executive Research Forum beginning in 1988 under a grant from the Bureau of Justice Assistance. The grant funded a Problem-Oriented Approach to Drug Enforcement project which was designed to test an application of analytical techniques to solving community drug problems. At the outset of that project, no one realized that police would be so interested and specifically concerned about drug problems in public housing communities. But the interest and dedication of police participating in the project — from Atlanta, Tampa, Tulsa, Philadelphia and, to a lesser degree, San Diego — helped PERF identify the need for a book about public housing as a guide for police dealing with drug-related problems. Their work in this area was valuable.

I appreciate the substantive feedback of all of the housing and criminal justice experts who reviewed this document. These individuals include Jim Armstrong and Judi Frist-Riutort of the Hampton (VA) Redevelopment Authority; Ned Symes and Kathleen Rotondaro of Quadel Consulting Corp. in Washington; Roosevelt Profit, chief of security for the Atlanta Housing Authority; Bill Armstead, from HUD's regional office in San Francisco; Debbie Greenstein, HUD Office of Policy Development and Research in Washington; Dave Hayeslip, a visiting fellow at the National Institute of Justice; and Major Carolyn Robison of the Tulsa Police Department.

I also appreciate the support and input from my colleagues, John Stedman and Diane Hill, and from John Eck, associate director for research for PERF.

This publication is dedicated to the police who work in public housing with dedication, persistence, and faith, who care about and respect the residents, and who use their analytical skills to solve problems and tap all kinds of resources to improve the lives of the people who reside there. You know who you are.

I.

Introduction

For more than 50 years, the federal government has taken an active role to ensure that low cost housing is available to the nation's poor families. Various programs and policies have been adopted and abandoned over the years. Some of these programs have been successful, others have been less so. The net result of the federal effort has been to provide some housing that often consists of very dense, sometimes poorly constructed or maintained dwelling units commonly known as "The Projects." For many Americans, these complexes stand as a symbol for a variety of social and crime problems.

The long-term effect of the nation's policies for housing the poor has in fact served to further concentrate the chronically poor in environments that can heighten both their social and economic problems. For example, in public housing, which is government's most direct provision of housing to the poor, the heads of household have many social and economic problems. These residents are mostly female, single parents and unemployed; they have little formal education and are mostly dependent on welfare to care for their children. In troubled public housing developments, the neighborhoods are unstable, isolated from many community services and job opportunities, often home to high crime, and segregated by minority groups. Each of these problems is directly related to poverty (U.S. HUD, 1980).

Because of these social and economic characteristics, law enforcement agencies have been confronted with a number of crime-related problems within troubled public housing complexes.

The high density of many developments — with up to 250 units in each of three 25-story buildings in one city and a two-mile strip of 28 16-story buildings in another — has complicated the role of police. Preventive patrolling in cars, for example, does nothing to deter drug dealing that takes place in the stairwells or jammed elevators of high-rise buildings. And when dwellings are not well built or designed, or in run-down condition, a number of crime-linked problems arise — flimsy doors and windows make residents easy victims of burglaries, lack of adequate lighting poses security problems and contributes to fear, and some buildings or complexes lack security measures (such as controlled entrance) that may be necessary to exclude troublemakers. The deteriorated physical environments — including as broken windows, trash-strewn grounds, and graffiti-riddled walls — have led to further deterioration.

The deteriorated physical conditions have contributed to the heightened sense of fear among the law-abiding residents of the complexes. Indeed, when researchers have explored the causes of fear, they have determined that environmental cues, such as vacant or abandoned housing, vandalism, vacant lots, litter, lack of upkeep and other physical evidence, groups loitering on corners, drinking and drug use in public, are more important than crime itself (Taylor, 1982: 294). These are the very characteristics which describe some of the nation's troubled public housing.

Violence is also high in the troubled public housing areas. Indeed, research in Chicago and Tulsa has shown that the highest rates of violent crime occur in poor,

2

minority-dominated communities (W.J. Wilson, 1987: 25; Allen, 1989). Part of the violence is linked with the volatility of aggressive drug dealing competition in these communities, as dealers engage in turf battles. Violence is also used by dealers against residents as an instrument of fear, or as a means to intimidate or injure police officers who work the areas. Sometimes, tragically, the violence affects innocent bystanders.

Both law enforcement officers and residents of these communities point to the high incidence of crime in the neighborhoods, especially of drug dealing and drug-related property or violent crimes. These crime problems contribute to a paralyzing fear among residents, police and other service providers. Those very fears encourage the escalation of drug activity.

For housing agency personnel, the drug problem has been manifested in a variety of problems including a significant reduction in rent collections; higher evictions of tenants for rent failure; and funding shortfalls that have affected physical appearances by forcing deferred maintenance.

For police, the key by-product of drug problems in public housing has been a resounding public call to resolve, at any cost, the problems in those communities. Many police agencies have responded to the mandate with more manpower, more resources, and more arrests, yet little has been accomplished to resolve the problems.

Traditionally, interagency cooperation between police and housing authorities has been limited. Part of that tradition dates back to the turbulent 1960s when racial rioting pitted black citizens against mostly white police officers. The riots caused havoc in public housing, and police were criticized because of their aggressive responses. Racial tensions were seriously exacerbated during the period.

It was only during the 1970s that the relationship between minority groups and police improved somewhat. Minorities had made strides in achieving parity through passage of civil rights legislation. Police developed and implemented specific policies and procedures more responsive to communities, especially minority communities. In particular, the absence of minorities on police departments was actively addressed. As a result, tensions eased, but the problems were never fully resolved.

In fact, it has become increasingly apparent a decade later that racial tensions and poverty, so dominant in public housing, have heightened the vulnerability of public housing residents, who are predominantly minorities, to crime-related problems — especially those linked to street level drug dealing.

Street level drug dealing in public housing has driven law-abiding residents to become de facto hostages within their own dwellings, has fostered youth becoming adjuncts in the drug trade, has encouraged welfare mothers to shelter drug dealers from the law, and contributed to many residents becoming drug abusers. Each of these by-products of drug dealing in public housing poses significant problems for both police and public housing officials.

Welfare mothers who abuse drugs often don't pay their rent; drug abusers, unable to afford treatment costs, may turn to property crime to sustain their addiction; law-abiding residents who don't venture outside can't participate in the vital role of helping to keep their neighborhood safe; and the youths who participate in the drug trade sacrifice their future to insulate the drug dealers from criminal sanctions.

These problems related to drug dealing have created common ground for police and public housing staff to work together in the 1980s and '90s. Because both local

4

housing officials and police are increasingly being held accountable by the public and elected officials for crime problems in these low income housing areas, each must take an active and collaborative role to address the problems.

From the police perspective, it is becoming increasingly clear that traditional policing strategies, such as preventive patrol and responding only to calls for service, will have little enduring impact in the troubled public housing communities. To be effective in handling drug problems in public housing, police must rethink their mission. If police officials are committed to making an impact on drug-related problems within public housing complexes, this task can be undertaken by police officers in any community. In order to accomplish this objective, police must develop a clear understanding of the workings of the local public housing authorities or agencies (PHAs) which manage public housing complexes.

In fact, the purpose of this monograph is to provide a working guide for police to develop an understanding of the PHAs and the public housing environment. It is intended to provide a springboard for establishing cooperative ventures that can serve to benefit the police agency, the local housing authority, the residents served in public housing communities, and the entire city's population.

By learning about public housing — the tenancy, the organization of housing, the funding mechanism, the politics — it may be easier for police to develop initiatives, in cooperation with these groups, to deal with drug problems. For example, knowing that the tenancy of a public housing building is elderly and that most of the crime consists of purse snatches and burglaries suggests a different police initiative than would be necessary for a high-rise complex occupied by families. Learning about the eviction and screening processes for public housing might suggest appropriate police roles. For example, in some cities, police assist housing agencies in routinely screening applicants for criminal records. Other police agencies routinely provide housing personnel with arrest reports for residents.

Just as police operate within a specialized environment, with rules and regulations that control the actions of officers, so does public housing. But for police officials who expand their knowledge of public housing and its operations, and develop cooperative relationships with housing officials and residents, opportunities exist to work together to solve problems. In areas where this type of collaborative relationship has occurred, results are encouraging.

It is important to recognize that public housing is really much like any other housing in the city. The residents and staff face a somewhat more complex set of problems that are often manifested in ways that demand police attention. Indeed, although this monograph is directed at addressing the needs of public housing, many of the techniques can be applied to any low income area of a city. The problems are much the same.

It is also important to accept that the problems related to poverty and racism and the vulnerability of public housing citizens are deeply-ingrained social problems that police cannot solve. However, police can identify and address components of these larger problems and make substantive progress in resolving them. That police involvement may take the form of improving the quality of life in a specific neighborhood, or deterring youth from involvement in drug activity; of restoring a sense of order to a drug corner, or shutting down a crack house. It could mean getting the lighting improved in a community, or having abandoned automobiles towed. And it may mean restoring control of the community to the law-abiding citizens who call public housing home. All of these are important accomplishments in battling community drug problems. When police and housing residents and staff can work together to tackle these problems constructively, there is an opportunity for a real and sustained management of the problems at the neighborhood level.

II.

Housing the Poor:
An Historical Perspective

Slums and poverty in urban settings have been a problem since agrarian cultures began to convert to industrial societies. As early as the 1800s, the American people began to be concerned about slums, chiefly because of health problems associated with poor sanitary conditions. These concerns primarily developed following the Civil War, when high unemployment, low wages, poor housing and working conditions gave rise to a broader concern about the welfare of people, particularly in the cities. Social reform at the turn of the century was tied to improving working conditions and public health in the struggle against poverty (W.J. Wilson, 1987: 165).

By 1882, the American government had expressed some limited concern about slum and tenement conditions. Congress appropriated a small amount of money to investigate the conditions which existed in the slum areas. Local government interest was limited during this period to establishing health and safety codes for housing in some cities (Arnold, 1982: 23).

Not until the early 1930s and the depths of housing shortages during the Great Depression did the government take an active role in housing. The first efforts were related to stimulating the private housing industry and helping individual homeowners. Not until 1937, with the passage of the landmark Housing Act, did the federal government set up a permanent system to provide local governments with the means to remedy poor housing conditions and provide "decent, safe and sanitary dwellings for families of low income" (Arnold, 1982: 27).

At the time conventional public housing was launched, the federal government began to finance the construction of apartment complexes to house, not the nation's poor families, but middle-class families who had been displaced by the depth of the economic depression that hit America during the 1930s. Fewer than 160,000 public housing units were built during the next decade following enactment of the Housing Act (Meehan, 1985: 291). The conditions of private housing during the decades of the 1930s and '40s remained inadequate for many citizens. These deficiencies continued partly because resources were diverted for the war; consequently construction of new homes and maintenance of existing homes had been deferred. By 1946, an estimated 40 percent of homes in the United States were still in dilapidated condition or lacked indoor plumbing; another 10 percent were overcrowded. These continued poor conditions led to the Housing Act of 1949, which kicked off construction of more public housing units.

Following World War II, the country had begun a path toward greater economic prosperity. By the 1950s, most Americans were enjoying a relative degree of prosperity. Most Americans significantly improved the quality of their housing during this period, and many Americans fulfilled the dream of owning their own home. In fact, during this period, many tenants moved out of the public housing complexes.

The housing lot of all families, however, was not improved. Blacks especially continued at a disadvantage in the housing markets and increasingly occupied the public housing complexes in urban centers. Over the

9

Southwark Plaza in Philadelphia was built in 1964 and consists of three 25-story towers and 26 two- and three-story buildings on 14.28 acres.

Seminole Hills in Tulsa was built in 1969 and has 250 units.

next years, the complexes increasingly housed a much poorer tenancy — a tenancy which had complex social problems and, because they were poor, few resources for solving their problems.

During those years, the public housing communities suffered financial difficulties and became a testimony to failed federal housing policies: "Public housing programs designed to help the big-city poor had suffered visible failures: huge structures rose above cityscapes like faceless warehouses, and with the passage of time, the communities clustered within them were demoralized, blighted by crime, and frustrated by the failure of their expectations" (President's Commission on Housing, 1982: xix).

By the 1960s, the government was increasingly turning away from the practice of directly providing public housing to the poor. Instead the government

College Hill Homes in Tampa consists of 710 apartments adjacent to an additional 700 units in another complex.

11

increasingly opted to provide additional housing to low-income families through the private sector. The government developed a market-like housing system using subsidies and tax incentives.

Today's conventional public housing was authorized by the Low-Rent Public Housing Program of 1937, which constitutes a significant portion of housing for poor families in this country. Nearly 200,000 public housing units were built during the first 12 years following enactment of the housing law. The federal commitment to public housing construction continued during the next decades: some 350,000 public housing units were built during the 1950s; 460,000 units during the '60s; and 385,000 units during the '70s.

The nation's current stock of more than a million public housing units is located all over the country although public housing is more typical of low income housing on the East Coast and in large cities. In more urban settings, these units are often high-rise buildings; less urban areas generally have public housing that consists of single- or two-story barrack-like dwelling units or townhouses. For most of today's police officers, the "housing projects" have always been there — a symbol of poverty and crime, often confined to specific areas within the city.

There are some 3,100 public housing authorities which provide conventional public housing for 1.4 million American families. This amount is less than 1.5 percent of the total housing stock in the country. There are some 32 million poor people in the nation, which is about one of every seven people (National Housing Task Force, 1988: 36). Some three and a half million of those poor — about 10 percent — are housed in the nation's public housing complexes. Millions of other poor families receive rental assistance through other housing programs subsidized by the government.

III.

Public Housing — Up Close

Residents and housing stock

Who lives in public housing? Generally, the
residents are among the poorest of the nation's poor.
The public housing program is designed to provide
housing for "lower-income" families. But public
housing agencies, which administer public housing, have
the discretion to set income limits for eligibility (in
accordance with state law). Thus income of tenants can

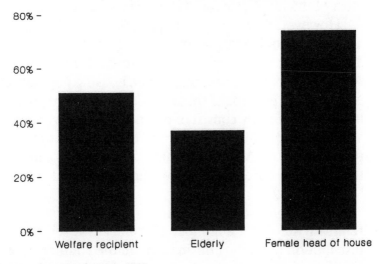

Characteristics of
Public Housing Residents

Source: The Urban Institute, 1979

13

vary from city to city and some public housing complexes do provide homes to a wide variety of incomes. For example, in Hampton, VA, a family of four can earn $24,950 and still be eligible for public housing.

The reality, however, is that almost all public housing residents are poor. Among public housing families, income averages 28 percent of the median national family income. In 1979, gross household income for public housing residents was an average $5,033 while the poverty line stood at $5,500 (Loux and Sadacca, 1979: 14; W. Wilson, 1987: 171). (Unfortunately, descriptive data about public housing residents as a group is a decade old. For a number of years, local housing agencies have not been required to report this information. A database is being developed in 1990 to capture this data.)

Prevailing images about the demographic composition of public housing are relatively accurate. Three-fifths of residents are minorities, many are single-parent families mostly headed by females and most of the families have at least several children.

However, there is also a large elderly population housed in public housing complexes, and the demographic characteristics are different for this group. About 37 percent of the total public housing population is elderly: 60 percent of these residents are white, their households usually consist of one person, the average age is 74, and nearly 40 percent of these households receive welfare. As with the family households, about three-quarters are headed by women (Loux and Sadacca, 1979).

The nation's stock of public housing has been relatively stable for a number of years. However, the distribution of public housing around the country varies significantly from region to region. Public housing is

DISTRIBUTION OF PUBLIC HOUSING
PERCENT BY FEDERAL REGION

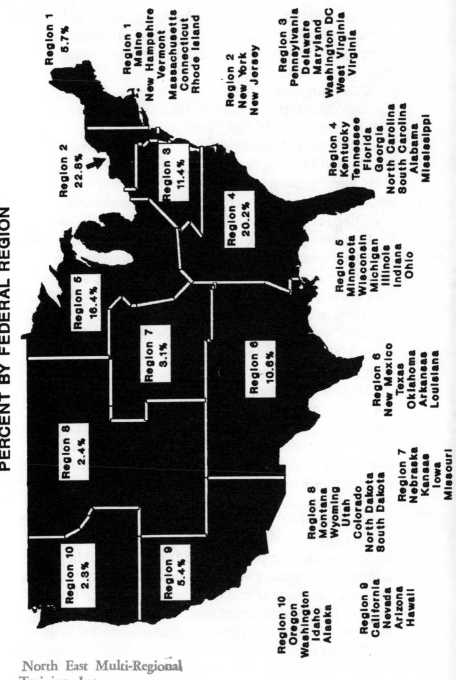

Region 1
5.7%

Region 1
Maine
New Hampshire
Vermont
Massachusetts
Connecticut
Rhode Island

Region 2
New York
New Jersey

Region 3
Pennsylvania
Delaware
Maryland
Washington DC
West Virginia
Virginia

Region 2
22.8%

Region 3
11.4%

Region 4
20.2%

Region 4
Kentucky
Tennessee
Florida
Georgia
North Carolina
South Carolina
Alabama
Mississippi

Region 5
Minnesota
Wisconsin
Michigan
Illinois
Indiana
Ohio

Region 5
16.4%

Region 7
3.1%

Region 6
10.6%

Region 6
New Mexico
Texas
Oklahoma
Arkansas
Louisiana

Region 8
2.4%

Region 7
Nebraska
Kansas
Iowa
Missouri

Region 8
Montana
Wyoming
Utah
Colorado
North Dakota
South Dakota

Region 10
2.3%

Region 9
5.4%

Region 9
California
Nevada
Arizona
Hawaii

Region 10
Oregon
Washington
Idaho
Alaska

North East Multi-Regional
Training, Inc.
1 Smoke Tree Plaza, Suite 111
North Aurora, IL 60542

15

concentrated in the northeast and south; New York City alone, with 174,000 public housing units, administers more than 10 percent of the nation's public housing stock (Bratt, 1986: 345).

Other large cities with public housing include: Chicago, 38,600 public housing units; Philadelphia, 22,900; Baltimore, 16,200; New Orleans, 13,600; Boston, 12,800; Washington, D.C., 11,200; Detroit, 10,300; and Los Angeles, with 8,220. But not all large cities have as much public housing. For example, two large cities without any conventional public housing are San Diego and San Jose (Struyk and Blake, 1982: 10).

Common perceptions about concentrations of public housing are not entirely accurate. Despite some regional concentration in the northeast, the rest of the nation's public housing is relatively dispersed. Fully one-third of the nation's public housing stock is operated by the 22 largest public housing agencies (of some 3,000) in the country; the remaining PHAs operate less than 6,500 units each.

Slightly more than half of the nation's public housing complexes are considered small, housing fewer than 200 families. Most public housing units for families (about 75 percent) are in low-rise buildings of less than five stories. Only 7 percent of family public housing complexes are both tall and large, despite the durable image of the nation's looming large public housing complexes (Bratt, 1986: 344).

So there is a fairly wide diversity among public housing stock. Complexes range from small public housing developments with less than 12 units to huge projects with more than 1,000 units. And design features vary from those complexes built in the 1930s and '40s in the East to newer complexes built in the late 1970s in the Southwest.

Much of public housing has become seriously deteriorated over the years. By 1988, Abt Associates, a consulting firm, estimated that the cost of correcting the backlog of identified physical deficiencies in the nation's 11,000 public housing complexes would be $9.3 billion for capital repairs and replacements (Bain et al., 1988: xi). Following that study, the federal housing agency reported that nearly 6 percent of the nation's public housing had "reached such a condition that it cannot be effectively or efficiently rehabilitated" (U.S. HUD, 1988b). To understand how public housing got in that condition, it is useful to explore the political and financial environment in which public housing operates.

Political/administrative structure

The programs that provide housing to poor families are run on the local level by Public Housing Agencies or Authorities known as PHAs. An "authority" is a legal term for a quasi-governmental organization created by a state legislature with some accountability to the local government. The important element of a housing authority is that it is created specifically for the purpose of administering a public housing program. Authorities have powers which cities and counties do not. For example, authorities can sell bonds for the construction of public housing and other redevelopment activity.

There are several types of PHAs which vary according to the area of their jurisdiction. Most have a city as their jurisdiction but there are some county or regional housing authorities. In addition to operating their own public housing complexes, some housing authorities also manage public housing units owned by the cities or states. Some states, such as New York, Massachusetts and Connecticut, have their own public housing programs (Bratt, 1986: 361).

Direction and advice from the local government and community is obtained informally through the authority's board of commissioners or directors and through public meetings. Local governments, such as city councils and county commissions, usually have no direct control of a PHA's activities.

The original intent of Congress in adopting this political structure for public housing was to leave control over housing to the locality through the authority. The plan was intended to counteract public and private resistance to the notion of government-financed housing. Government financing of housing was largely unpopular in the '30s.

Because of their intergovernmental organizational structure and funding process, PHAs have a number of different masters. First, PHAs are typically headed by a volunteer Board of Commissioners, or Directors, who are responsible for insuring that the authority is operated according to sound business practices and principles (U.S. HUD, n.d.). The commissioners are typically appointed by the city's chief executive officer; they are not elected by the citizens (Arnold, 1982: 28). The full board of directors (or commissioners) takes formal actions by approving resolutions which become part of the official records and policy for the authority.

In general, the boards of commissioners are responsible for duties such as establishing rent schedules and income limits for new tenants (which the federal government must approve), approving annual budgets, and handling other management-related matters. The board is also responsible for hiring a paid executive director who handles the day-to-day management of the authority's programs. In a small housing program, the executive director will also be a housing manager; larger authorities have on-site managers for operating large complexes. Managers are responsible for rent collection, tenant relations, bookkeeping and accounting, repairs and maintenance (U.S. HUD, n.d.).

The board of directors is only one of the masters of the PHA. The U.S. Department of Housing and Urban Development (known as HUD) is a huge federal agency with an annual budget of more than $14.9 billion. A major part of HUD's responsibility is to provide housing subsidies for low income families. In that role, HUD maintains control over many of the actions of the board members of PHAs. Standards for apartment space, cross ventilation, recreation, density and so forth are set by HUD. And Congress requires HUD to establish income limits for admission, criteria for continued occupancy, and rental schedules. The goal is

ORGANIZATION FOR PUBLIC HOUSING

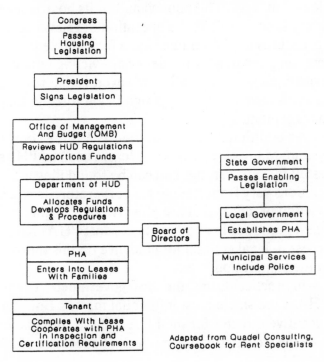

Adapted from Quadel Consulting, Coursebook for Rent Specialists

19

that HUD help insure the solvency of each authority and a degree of equity across the country. HUD circulates rules that govern the operations of PHAs (see attached organizational chart). It is important to note that HUD also controls much of the money that is received by the local PHAs to subsidize the low-income tenants. And HUD is accountable both to the U.S. Congress and to the President who appoints the Secretary of HUD.

Another master for the PHA is the tenant or resident council of the authority. In the late 1960s and '70s, tenant rights were expanded in response to views by residents that management was often insensitive to the needs of tenants. But statutes and court decisions specified that "tenants were entitled to ... a voice in the management of development affairs" (Meehan, 1985: 308). Tenant councils consist of residents with officers elected at large. This council and/or its board may have a very specific role in the operation of grievance procedures and sometimes has a formal role in screening tenants for residency or evicting tenants from the complexes. The reality, however, is that resident councils have rarely been a significant force in shaping management.

An additional master for the PHA is the court system. Many of the rules and leases used by PHAs are tested in court settings and can be found illegal. Court opinions vary from state to state; therefore leases or eviction practices that are effective in one state may be ruled improper in another state. Most PHAs have access to legal counsel for guidance on this thorny area of their operations.

In practical terms, the local government for the PHA is the single most influential master. Both the executive director for the PHA and the commissioners take their cues from the city's chief executive officer and city council. In fact, the quality and style of the operation of the PHA tends to reflect the style of local government.

Financing and Management of PHAs

As with many organizations, understanding the funding process for PHAs, and its historical development, provides insight into the operations. For public housing, the last three decades tell an important story.

The original funding scheme for public housing authorities was such that the federal government assumed full capital costs, that is, the principal and interest of bonds floated by the local authorities. Tenants were charged only enough rent to cover operating expenses. Those operating expenses included maintenance and administration with debt service excluded from these local costs. The role of local governments was to provide basic services such as public safety and sanitation.

The construction of public housing has been funded through the sale of tax-exempt notes and bonds with the federal government paying the principal and interest payments. HUD would then sell the debt contracts on behalf of PHAs to private investors, such as banks and insurance companies, and use the proceeds to pay for interest and principal. (There has been little new construction of public housing in recent years.)

Through the early years of public housing, during the 1930s and '40s when public housing served a middle class population, the rents collected from tenants were adequate to cover operating expenses. But over time, the federal government increasingly specified which tenants public housing must accommodate. Those tenant guidelines began in the early 1950s. At that time, housing agencies were required to house families displaced by urban renewal and were authorized to evict higher income families. The federal government later restricted public housing to the very low income, that is, to those tenants who could afford to pay only the very least amount of rent. Thus the operating revenues collected by PHAs fell dramatically.

From the program's inception through 1961, rent remained the sole source of income for the local housing authorities. In that year, the federal government began to provide regular, if inadequate, subsidies to PHAs. These subsidies were very limited and directed only to the elderly and some other special groups. They were too small to halt the slide in operating revenues being experienced by PHAs (Meehan, 1985: 303).

The shoestring budgets under which PHAs operated in the 1960s caused properties to become seriously deteriorated. For example, in Boston, the housing authority began cutting into its savings (reserves) for operating funds. This deficit financing for Boston's authority contributed to accelerated deterioration. The deterioration associated with deferred maintenance and eroded morale caused "financial and social problems...to pile up for the future." Among the authority's problems were literally thousands of broken windows, basic difficulties with heating and sewer systems, and a demand from tenants to provide a community-controlled security force (Peattie, 1972: 5).

In 1968, the housing act increased the financial burden on PHAs by requiring social services, additional private security guards, and recreational equipment. Again, those services were to be provided exclusively from rental income (Meehan, 1985: 304).

PHAs had originally attempted to make up their revenue shortfall by charging higher rents. But the federal government did away with that option in 1969 by limiting the rent that could be charged to any tenant to 25 percent of adjusted income. (The percentage cap now is 30 percent.) The move was an effort to protect tenants from having to pay too much of their income for rent. But as inflation continued to drive up operating costs, relative income for the PHAs fell dramatically.

It became increasingly clear that HUD had to provide substantial monetary subsidies or housing authorities would simply go broke. In 1971, HUD did just that. But despite the financial assistance from HUD, some authorities were too deeply troubled to fully recover. The most notably troubled was the beleaguered Boston Housing Authority, which went into receivership. HUD subsidies for operating expenses continued to climb throughout the 1970s but declined during the years of the Reagan administration.

Further restrictions on the ability of PHAs to generate enough rent to cover costs occurred during the 1980s. First, PHAs were required to eliminate rent ceilings that had helped the PHA keep higher income tenants in public housing. During this decade, HUD also reduced the income limits for new tenants (which contributed to the growth of a poorer tenancy) and federal preferences were established which mandated the selection of the tenants with physical, economic and other problems.

Because of all the federal mandates, PHAs continued to encounter financial difficulties. By 1988, the average public housing unit required an annual subsidy of $1,200 (National Housing Task Force, 1988: 39). That is, it costs the federal government about $100 per month per public housing unit to keep local public housing afloat, despite the desire of the federal agency that public housing be self-supporting.

Not only did HUD come through with operating subsidies for public housing in the early 1970s, but

HUD also provided some modernization funds for capital replacement and equipment — $1.7 billion in 1981 and 1982, and $2.5 billion in 1983. But these funds were very limited relative to the backed-up needs of public housing. Many of the resources were earmarked for specific uses that may not have been priorities for the PHA which received the money (Bratt, 1986: 340).

Across the country, public housing authorities over the years have earned a reputation for being poorly managed. That perception is based largely upon the financial troubles of a few housing agencies. But PHA supporters argue that the financial conditions have occurred because of federal mandates for service, rent setting and income ceilings, and other policies without funds to make up the difference.

Although public housing was intended to be locally owned and operated, since the 1940s, federal control has increased markedly. "Federal law and regulations now extend in significant detail into virtually every aspect of PHA ownership and operations" (President's Commission on Housing, 1982: 31). Over the years, HUD had specifically imposed four large financial burdens on the PHAs for public housing. Utility costs were to be included in rent; 10 percent of gross income from rent less utility costs had to be paid to local governments (in lieu of taxes); cash reserves were limited; and any "profits" earned were required to be repaid to HUD to reduce annual supplements (Meehan, 1985: 296-7).

Some local housing officials claim the presence of these burdensome federal regulations "explains why public housing fell into disrepute after 30 years of successful operations." They further claim that although some housing authorities have been troubled, the criticism should not be directed to all public housing operations (Kuhn, 1988: 67).

Others argue that the federal government set public housing up for financial failure through financing only capital expenses, and setting caps on the ability of PHAs to set rents and maintain surplus funds. HUD took away any market-like incentives to be efficient; PHAs were forced to minimize their income by housing only the poorest tenants. Then ceilings were put on the percentage of the resident's income that could be collected for rent. The policy had the effect of minimizing the amount of rent PHAs could collect. This policy contrasts with the rent-maximizing method in which private landlords conduct their business. In addition, PHAs were penalized if they were efficient. Thus, if operating revenues increased, federal subsidies were reduced. HUD's subsidy system is based upon performance by the PHA. The operating expense level is calculated and HUD covers the spread between rent collection and expenses.

One problem is that HUD's formula for calculating expense levels may be inadequate and some PHAs have great difficulty with rent collection among their tenants. PHAs often don't collect what HUD calculates they should. The bottom line is that many PHAs have financial difficulties.

Operations:
Eligibility, Screening and Evictions

Eligibility

Within the public housing system in a city, there are likely to be both "good" and "bad" complexes. The bad ones are sometimes known as "federal slums," while the desirability of living in the good projects is attested to by the efforts of families to gain entry to these complexes. Long waiting lists can signal a well-run complex. Indeed, the desirability of a complex within a city may be estimated by its vacancy rate as compared to the vacancy rates of other public housing complexes within the city (Peattie, 1972: 7). The availability of low cost private housing in the rental market can also have an impact on vacancies. Other factors such as the ability of the housing agency to make the apartment ready for occupancy, maintenance funds, and how quickly PHAs learn about vacancies also affect the vacancy rates in complexes.

To get into public housing, families must apply to their public housing authority. The application is evaluated by the authority's staff based upon criteria related to income, need, and other factors. Despite the general description of public housing residents, a prospective resident does not need to be a minority or female to be admitted to public housing. In fact, to get into public housing, a prospective resident need not even be poor. The only income requirement (from HUD) is that applicants generally earn less than 80 percent of the median income for the area. (HUD encourages the PHA to house a mix of income levels.) PHAs, however, can establish more rigid income requirements and other criteria which applicants must meet.

If the family is determined eligible, they are typically placed upon the housing authority's waiting list. As units become available in the public housing complex, the family in its turn will be assigned to a unit (U.S. HUD, 1982). But it can be a very slow process. The average wait to get into public housing in major cities is 21 months (Shapiro, 1989). Many people wait much longer.

There are federal preferences, however, requiring PHAs to give priority to the homeless and displaced families, and those living in substandard housing. In certain cases, where a PHA is under a HUD- or court-ordered mandate, federal preferences must be followed in order to meet racial quotas.

Despite what might appear to be a large number of public housing units, many housing authorities, such as Baltimore's, have long waiting lists. In New York City, the waiting list exceeds more than 200,000 families who want to join the city's 600,000 public housing tenants. Compounding the problem in New York is the fact that turnover of units is less than 4 percent annually (Duggan, 1988).

Many other cities also have long waiting lists. In Newark, NJ, the public housing authority had more than 11,000 names on a waiting list but stopped taking applications in 1988. The authority has 12,225 public housing units; about 40 percent were vacant or uninhabitable in 1988 (Kurtz, 1988).

The vacancy rates in public housing aren't just a problem in a few cities. All told, in 1988, there were some 840,000 families on waiting lists for public housing across the nation (Shapiro, 1989: 20).

Screening

Each public housing authority decides (within federal guidelines) exactly who will live in its public housing. Consequently, the tenant population varies from city to city, and for each complex. One big city public housing development for families is John Hope Homes in Atlanta, a community of 606 units housing 1,070 residents. The residents of John Hope Homes had the following characteristics in 1988:

- 99.55 percent of all residents were black
- 65.10 percent of the residents were female (many of the males were dependent children living with their mothers)
- 40 percent of the residents were ages 18 - 49, 42 percent were under age 18

- 69 percent of the residents had family incomes of less than 5,000 (Atlanta Housing Authority, 1988)

However, there has been a relatively wide variance among characteristics of residents in public housing across the nation. In a study, some 54 percent of Los Angeles public housing tenants were black, but 90 percent of Philadelphia tenants were black; 26 percent of Atlanta's tenants were over age 65, but only 11 percent in Los Angeles were over that age. In Atlanta, 90 percent of public housing families were headed by single parents, while 76 percent were single parents in Baltimore (Struyk and Blake, 1982: 1).

In looking at four large public housing agencies on the East Coast, Struyk and Blake found a wide range of other characteristics. For example, in one PHA, 59 percent of residents had income below $3,000 (1979 data), while only 10 percent of another PHA's residents

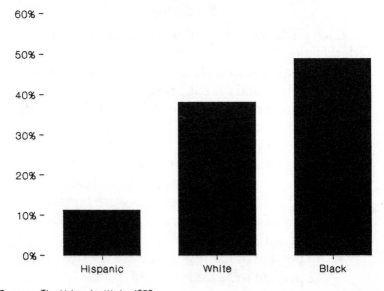

Race of Public Housing Residents

Source: The Urban Institute, 1979

had incomes that low. Similarly, among those four PHAs, a job was the major source of income for 55 percent of residents at one; at another PHA, only 6 percent had jobs (Struyk and Blake, 1982).

It is clear that public housing residents vary widely. The first question one might ask is why do these variations exist? One major reason for the variation is the difference in screening practices and admissions policies at different PHAs.

Each PHA determines its own admissions strategy. Admissions strategies for housing authorities can be discerned by looking at three different elements. First, in conjunction with family size, how does the PHA define income and the income limit that residents must meet to be admitted to public housing? (Note that HUD must approve these income limits.) Second, what assets may residents have and still be admitted to public housing? Third, what are the PHA's priorities for admission?

These priorities for admission vary from housing authority to housing authority. For example, Atlanta Housing Authority gives a priority to battered women with children who are leaving a violent relationship. HUD does give local housing agencies the right to set admission policies. But HUD does specify some factors that may and may not be be considered relevant in deciding who gets into public housing. For example, PHAs may consider whether an applicant has a bad rent payment history, conviction for violent criminal behavior, bad history as a tenant, bad history of housekeeping or a household head who is a minor. However, the PHA must consider the "individual circumstances, justifications or rehabilitation."

The point about reviewing individual circumstances is important. For example, in considering an applicant's criminal record, the "Authority must be willing to consider evidence that the applicant has changed or has been rehabilitated. In other words, a robbery conviction five years ago is insufficient by itself to preclude admission to public housing. However, the burden of proof or rehabilitation rests with the applicant; and the PHA need not solicit such proof. Thus, in many instances, an Authority is able to reject an applicant on the grounds of unacceptable behavior in the past, as long as such behavior is adequately documented" (Stuyk and Blake, 63)

HUD also prohibits several other factors from being considered by PHAs in the screening process. These factors include welfare status, adequacy of income, marital status, cohabitation, being a student, sexual preference, arrest record, ability to speak English, and/or having foster children (Struyk and Blake, 1982: 65). Of course, housing authorities cannot discriminate with regard to race, sex, national origin, or religious preference. (A number of housing authorities in the 1980s, however, were still wrestling with the issue of desegregation. See Pereira, 1988, and Yen, 1988.)

Screening applicants on the basis of relevant factors is a time-consuming process and PHAs take varying approaches. For example, among the four large PHAs studied by Struyk and Blake, prospective residents were screened to varying degrees on the following criteria: Criminal record, rent-paying behavior, housekeeping, mental/physical disability, present housing condition, and reason for moving and record of performance as a public housing resident. In three of the four PHAs, police regularly provided the PHA with information on criminal records (Struyk and Blake, 1982: 15).

In some housing authorities, the screening process is more extensive than in other developments. For example, in Baltimore, a specific office of the housing authority is responsible for both application and screening. The chief of that office and her staff conduct home visits and interview applicants to determine if the applicant "is capable of maintaining him or herself in a housing unit." In many other PHAs, neither time nor staff is available to conduct such extensive screening. And some PHAs interpret the federal regulations differently as to how much they can screen applicants and to what degree federal preferences must be accommodated (Venture for Quality Public Housing, 1988).

In a public housing complex in St. Louis, Cochran Gardens, prospective tenants are not only screened for housekeeping skills but also to determine whether the tenant has anyone designated to provide childcare for youths in the family. Although much time there is spent on screening, the complex has had success with getting tenants in place who comply with the rules. Screening here is conducted by a group of residents who also participate in an innovative resident management program.

In New York City's public housing, residency is denied to applicants who have histories of criminal or violent behavior (again, this is conviction, not arrest), or drug abuse. The screening includes a face-to-face eligibility interview and home visits. Applicants are asked to account for each member of the family, such as school attendance and employment history. Applicants are also asked about the arrest record, drug involvement and any rehabilitation of every family member. The information is verified by PHA staff (Popolizio, 1989).

Thus, it is clear that the tenancy of public housing varies widely around the country, and that PHAs have wide latitude in selecting their tenants. Those selection processes have important implications for the well-being of the public housing communities.

31

Evictions

Screening is an important dimension of the admissions process because once tenants occupy units of public housing, they can be forced to leave only through formal eviction processes. (It is important to note that tenants are not required to leave public housing if their income rises; they are only required to pay 30 percent of their income for rent, and they are required to report changes in their income.) Evictions from public housing are made on the basis of lease violations. By far the most common breach of the lease is for non-payment of rent. Other breaches may range from allowing more people than are named on the lease to occupy a dwelling, or having unreported income, to being convicted of a felony crime such as drug dealing. Since each PHA's lease is different, the lease enforcement and subsequent evictions vary widely from PHA to PHA.

Leases of PHAs are not all that different from the lease one might sign when renting a privately-owned apartment. (Several leases are included as an attachment.) These documents spell out who can occupy the unit and under what conditions, state the due date of payment for rent, explain rules and regulations for the complex, including use of the premises by guests, regulations about pets and so forth. The formal process of evicting a tenant is time consuming, and eviction processes vary from housing authority to housing authority. The guidelines for eviction are set forth by HUD but are affected by the landlord-tenant laws and judicial interpretation in each state. Local policies — both written and unwritten — also influence evictions. For example, HUD rules require that all PHA tenants are entitled to a grievance procedure before they are evicted. Grievance procedure requirements date back to times when many localities did not have due process included in landlord/tenant laws, so HUD set up its own process requirements. Now each housing authority has a written grievance procedure but policies do vary from one jurisdiction to another.

In early 1989, HUD was working to streamline procedures for evicting tenants for drug-related activities. HUD lawyers were reviewing eviction laws on a state-by-state basis to determine whether the laws in place adequately protected tenants. If the lawyers determined that tenants were adequately protected by the state's due process law (that is, the tenants could seek redress in court), HUD would permit waiver of the federal eviction procedures so that lawbreaking tenants could be evicted quickly by the PHA. Further information about this new policy should be forthcoming.

Despite the legal quagmire, some cities are able by practice to evict tenants fairly rapidly. In Atlanta, for example, upon felony arrest, tenants receive a notice to vacate their unit because they are in violation of their lease agreement. Although the residents are entitled to the formal grievance procedure, most of them voluntarily vacate the unit within the three days specified in the letter, according to the PHA's director of security. Eviction following arrest is an issue subject to interpretation and debate. Some call the process intimidation and unfair to low income residents. Others say that in today's climate of drug activity in public housing, a felony arrest is a good sign that the tenant is engaging in inappropriate behavior. Some PHAs interpret an arrest as evidence that a tenant's actions are threatening the safety and well-being of the other residents, thus clearly violating the lease agreement. A number of PHAs have rewritten their leases to clearly prohibit drug-related activity by tenants; this lease provision helps clarify the 'eviction upon arrest' issue.

In certain cities, the eviction process is cumbersome and the PHA is unable to evict tenants quickly. In Baltimore, for example, evictions may take up to a year because tenants routinely take advantage of grievance procedures (Venture for Quality Public Housing, 1988). In New York City, an extreme example but one which shows the extremes of the eviction issue, "Court-mandated procedures for insuring due process often has resulted in eviction cases being dragged out to two or three years (Popolizio, 1988)."

Under the court-mandated procedures, project managers in New York City

> "must first interview the tenant. If remedial action fails, or the manager believes termination to be appropriate, the case is then referred to the Authority's Office of Resident Review and Counseling. They review the case. If cause for termination exists, ORRC refers the matter to the Law Department. The Law Department will then prepare a "Notice of Charges" which is sent to the tenant. A full administrative hearing will be held before an impartial hearing officer. Witnesses may testify, evidence can be presented, cross-examination is permitted. The hearing officer prepares a written decision, which may be confirmed by the Authority's Board. If confirmed, that determination is served on the tenant. The Authority may now commence a holdover proceeding in the local Housing Court. It should be noted that our actions are often impeded by meritless appeals of the administrative decision. Judicial stays and appeals have delayed evictions for as long as two years. The entire process, from beginning to end, can sometimes take up to three years to complete" (Popolizio, 1989).

It is clearly the court-mandated process which makes New York's eviction process excessively long. However, the grievance procedures set forth by HUD specify that the PHA must first send the tenant a "notice of termination." That document must tell the tenant why he or she is being terminated, and of his or her right to reply and request a hearing before a grievance panel. Time periods are specified within which actions must occur. During 1988, the housing authority of New York tried a new technique for ousting errant tenants from its units. Federal marshals with court orders swooped down on two projects, arrested suspected drug dealers, seized their leases and started eviction procedures. Their efforts were sanctioned under the federal asset forfeiture law which permits the seizure of assets of drug dealers. This was the first occasion civil provisions of the federal drug laws had been used to seize public housing leases. This was an innovative application of asset forfeiture laws in that leases of rental property were considered to be assets of the leaseholder.

It is important to note that screening new residents and evicting aberrant ones are two important tools which PHAs can use to control occupancy and the behavior of residents. Both these processes require significant time and staff. In summary, despite the rules, there is tremendous variety among PHAs in:

- the level of enforcement of leases and rules
- the knowledge of eviction and screening techniques
- the staff resources and legal assistance available to use these methods
- the interpretation of HUD regulations

In some PHAs, thorough processes for screening, adequate leases and a process for monitoring behavior exist but the PHAs simply may not use these mechanisms to their fullest potential. HUD, for example, has recently encouraged PHAs to improve lease enforcement. The ability of PHAs to comply with that request can vary widely.

It is equally important to note that for years, most PHA evictions were for non-payment of rent. Any other lease violations were considered by the PHA as too difficult to prove. Historically PHAs had "refused to recognize that criminal conviction is not needed in an eviction proceeding because as landlords they are enforcing the lease (which is a civil action) not the law (which is a criminal action)." The inability and lethargy of management in evicting problem tenants led public housing to its current deteriorated condition (Brown, 1989).

Since the drug problems have heightened in public housing, however, most PHAs around the country are working to strengthen their leases and enforce these documents so that scofflaws, particularly those engaging in drug activity, can be evicted more quickly.

It is worth noting that PHAs are under pressure from HUD to keep up occupancy levels and tenant accounts receivable. For example, the Atlanta Housing Authority in 1988 was threatened with the loss of $700,000 in federal subsidies if an occupancy rate of 92 percent was not met. The occupancy goal was part of a five-year occupancy plan imposed on the agency by HUD. The authority must maintain occupancy at 97 percent by 1991 in order to continuing receiving the full HUD subsidy. The Atlanta Housing Authority responded to the deadline reportedly by recruiting families from the city's homeless shelters (Wells, 1988b).

It is not uncommon if demand for public housing, or certain housing complexes, is low, for PHAs to relax screening to keep occupancy rates up (in other words, to stay "leased up"). Strong lease enforcement may be interpreted by HUD as promoting vacancies and reducing the accounts receivable from tenants, at least in the short run.

Management Problems

Making ends meet has been a major problem for PHAs and has contributed to financial and management difficulties which have troubled many large PHAs. In 1983, HUD's inspector general declared that 30 of the largest PHAs, administering 23 percent of the nation's public housing units, were financially troubled or had failed to maintain adequate operating reserve funds. (Reserve funds are monies required to be set-aside for maintenance and other high ticket items. It is generally considered a sign of financial trouble when any organization spends its reserves to pay for day-to-day operating costs.)

Other PHAs have experienced problems with a variety of basic management issues. These issues include evictions, rent collection, tenant relations, maintenance and repairs (Bratt, 1986: 347).

Administrators for PHAs must also deal with three other complex management-related issues: (1) poorly designed and constructed dwellings, (2) security and crime issues, and (3) competing demands.

Poor design and construction

The first of these issues, poor design and construction of public housing, makes maintenance difficult and expensive for housing authorities. One critic described the construction during the post-war building boom: "The quality of building construction was often poor and sometimes grossly inadequate. Poor construction and inadequate resources for maintenance, reinforced by a social climate in which vandalism was sometimes positively encouraged rather than impeded, produced significantly accelerated deterioration of facilities in the 1960s" (Meehan, 1985: 291). According to Meehan, the common practice had been to pay "premium prices for apartments so shoddily built that a choir of angels could not have abided in them regularly without producing serious disrepair" (Meehan, 1985: 293).

Meehan believes that PHAs were financially gouged by the housing industry during those years. The poor construction, combined with years of neglect, contributed to accelerated deterioration. But the housing was so badly needed that only in rare cases were buildings actually demolished. (In 1988, a new federal law required that every unit of public housing demolished must be replaced on an equivalent basis, a scheme known as "one for one replacement" in order to ensure that the public housing stock was not reduced further (Kurtz, 1988).)

Poor design of public housing also contributed to the deterioration of the housing developments over the years. During the 1950s, with the increasing costs of urban land, public housing was constructed in the form of high-rise buildings, often clustered together. The result of this building pattern proved "dangerous to live in and costly to maintain" (Newman, 1973: 8). The dangers came from the reduced ability of residents to participate in surveillance of the property, lack of real or symbolic barriers (such as fences, gates, steps or plantings) that serve as territorial boundaries, and the social stigma associated with the appearance of these buildings. They were also poorly designed for families with children. These high-rise designs resulted in distinctly higher crime patterns in public housing (Newman, 1973). High-rise public housing thus became discredited over the years. In 1968, Congress prohibited housing families in high-rise buildings except in emergencies (Meehan, 1985: 307). Now most public housing families (75 percent) are housed in low-rise buildings (less than five stories) (Bratt, 1986: 344). High-rise buildings are used primarily to house elderly residents.

The current need for renovation of public housing thus comes partly from outmoded planning and design, deterioration from age, hard use, poor maintenance and interim patchwork improvements. Some public housing can be redesigned or renovated to improve both the design and the condition of the buildings. In some cases, after years of deterioration, housing has simply not been salvageable. In Newark, NJ, the authority demolished 816 apartments in 1987 and had plans to demolish nine more high rises. The head of Newark's housing authority believed those units could not be salvaged "no

University Homes in Atlanta is a 675-unit complex built in 1937. It is adjacent to another 606 units of public housing.

matter how much money [was] poured into them" (Kurtz, 1988).

Recognizing the need to invest in capital improvements, HUD started aprogram in 1981 known as the Comprehensive Improvement Assistance Program (CIAP) or Modernization Fund. (CIAP was an extension of the Modernization Program which has existed since the 1970s.) This program makes funds available for capital improvement of public housing. In Philadelphia, for example, $29 million of modernization funds in 1988-89 was slated (but delayed) to renovate three 25-story public housing buildings that have up to 250 units each. The cost per unit for renovations here and in other urban settings is steep. (For example, renovations at Kenilworth-Parkside in Washington, D.C., which is being converted to tenant ownership, are budgeted at an average cost of $49,600 per unit (Davidson, 1989a).) A portion of the renovation cost usually is earmarked for redesign of buildings to ease security-related problems. A study by HUD in early 1988 indicated that a total of more than $10 billion would be necessary to modernize the nation's public housing stock (National Housing Task Force, 1988: 37).

Security and Crime

The second management problem for PHAs, security, has been addressed in various ways by PHAs. A number of public housing authorities have launched their own security forces to police their complexes. The Baltimore Housing Authority created a Division of Security and Police Service in late 1986. The division arose from a realization of "the need for greater security in our public housing communities." In this Maryland city, all the PHA's officers are trained by the Baltimore City Police Department. The PHA security division also employs off-duty city police officers to patrol the PHA's facilities.

The goal of Baltimore's security force is to increase "the safety and security of residents and to protect physical improvements made in Housingauthority properties city-wide." These officers patrol properties, conduct investigations, and control access to high-rise buildings. Patrol is both random foot and motorized patrol, and what the organization calls "vertical patrol," that is, within high rise buildings (Venture for Quality Public Housing, 1988).

New York City's public housing authority, which manages 178,000 apartments, also has its own police force. With 2,000 officers, the force is larger than most municipal police departments. It is the nation's 19th largest police department (Duggan, 1988).

HUD specifically discourages authorities from having their own private security force. The housing department's perception is that an authority-operated security force only serves to reinforce the isolation of public housing communities from the benefits of city police protection that are provided to other citizens. Authority security forces may be improperly trained, and funding for their services can sometimes evaporate with little notice. HUD also feels a private security force minimizes local police interest in the protection of the public housing community (U.S. HUD, 1988d).

While it is true that many PHAs don't pay taxes to the city because they don't generate enough revenue, each PHA operates under a cooperative agreement with the city which includes a Payment in Lieu of Taxes scheme (PILOT). PILOT is 10 percent of gross rents collected less utility payments. HUD's view is that regardless of whether the PHA can make this payment, the city has agreed (through a cooperative agreement) to provide certain basic services. Those basic services, according to HUD, include full police protection. In fact, the 1937 Housing Act required local governments to provide such services as garbage collection, paving, lighting, police and fire services. But those obligations have been difficult to enforce. Many PHAs in the 1960s began to secure these services on their own, sometimes at the behest of angry tenants, at an increased cost of operations (Meehan, 1985: 292). (For a further description of the PHA's responsibilities, see Appendix B.)

HUD claims that inadequate local police coverage of public housing is a common security problem. This inadequate coverage, HUD says, results from three factors: "a community wide shortage of police manpower; a police assumption that the PHA security force, if any, will handle it; and police avoidance of public projects as too difficult and thankless" (Kolodny, Baron and Struyk, 1983a: 88).

Despite claims of poor municipal police service, in some cities, police invest a disproportional share of their time in policing low income communities. In Philadelphia, standard operating procedure is for three cars to respond to calls in one high rise public housing complex: one car takes the call, one car is a back-up, and one car watches the equipment to avoid acts of vandalism.

In Tampa, FL, police staffing for one public housing community is 5 percent of sworn strength to police an area that is populated by .95 percent of the city's residents (Tampa Police Dept., 1989).

Underreporting of crime may contribute to the crime problem in some public housing. Under some circumstances, residents may simply avoid calling the police. For example, residents have learned that a call to a 911-Enhanced dispatching system displays the address of the caller. If police show up at the caller's

42

door to obtain more information, residents fear retaliation from the people causing the trouble. In some Chicago housing complexes where gangs control residents through violence and intimidation, a police follow-up to the caller's apartment is a clear signal to gang members implicating the resident in the reporting of an incident (Kotlowitz, 1988).

Indeed, many residents cannot report crime because they don't have telephones or access to telephones. A community survey of selected public housing complexes in Tampa, Atlanta, Philadelphia and Tulsa revealed that from 31 to 62 percent of residents did not have a telephone in their apartment. Other residents reported they did not call the police because they felt nothing could or would be done by the police (Tampa Police Dept., 1989; Huguley, 1989; Meeks and Hasson, 1989; Allen, 1989).

Competing Demands

Public housing agencies have a difficult task balancing the competing demands imposed upon them. And these difficulties are ones which housing agencies commonly face in managing public housing programs. But public housing is only one responsibility for public housing agencies. (See Appendix A for a description of additional housing responsibilities for housing agencies.)

PHAs are accountable to different bosses with competing interests. As tenants have played an increasing role in the management of housing, the complexities of management have increased. Residents, management, and HUD have tended to be adversaries rather than partners. Thus, the very measures intended as safeguards to protect the interests of varied groups can serve to slow decision-making processes and subsequent actions.

Lack of a clear chain of command and accountability allows management problems to continue for long periods and get out of hand. Here is one accounting of the effects in the early 1980s of poor administration in a public housing environment: "Poor management by the Boston HousingAuthority created grim conditions in many developments. Disruptive tenants were seldom evicted and repairs went undone, with employees often doing no work at all. And because of political patronage, the housing authority became a deeply entrenched and isolated haven for the politically faithful" (Bratt, 1986: 347).

A national housing task force described the complex relationships that have contributed to the poor management of some PHAs: "Some local housing authorities, for example, have failed to manage projects efficiently and responsively. State and local governments too often have lacked the desire or the legal authority to correct housing authority failures. HUD and Congress have compounded these problems by failing to provide a predictable and reasonable level of operating support. Federal laws often have imposed rigid, costly requirements upon authorities, without providing the funding to meet them. HUD has lacked both the capacity and the will to deal with seriously nonperforming authorities" (National Housing Task Force, 1988: 37-38).

This task force recommended that HUD take control of the "handful of public housing projects in a few cities" where drugs and crime have fostered "domestic terrorism." The group urged that "control of these projects be removed from local authorities that have proven unable to deal with them. HUD should assume responsibility for project management, and Congress should appropriate whatever funds are necessary to enable HUD or an appointed receiver to do an effective job" (National Housing Task Force, 1988: 11).

PART TWO

Chapters 1-3 of this book discussed how PHAs work, including the politics, history and organizational dynamics of public housing. Beginning with Chapter 4, this book explores how drug problems have created a common ground for PHAs, police and tenants. The second half of this book thus explores how these shared problems can aid police in developing and implementing collaborative solutions in response to community drug problems.

IV.

Charting Common Ground

The dynamics of retail drug dealing have particularly harmful effects on poor communities. These effects can be very visible in some troubled public housing communities. Although there is a wide variance around the nation in the kind and degree of impact drugs have on public housing, retail drug dealing can both harm poor people as individuals and cause the poor community to become dysfunctional. A dysfunctional community seriously complicates the traditional role of police as enforcers of the law and keepers of the peace.

Police often face major difficulties in working in troubled public housing communities. An assignment to public housing can mean working in an environment populated by a socially and physically isolated group of residents with complex economic problems who live in housing administered by agencies that have limited resources and little political clout. And there may be a great deal of antagonism between police and residents.

It is these same characteristics which make public housing as a community and public housing residents as individuals particularly vulnerable to the harmful effects of drug dealing activity.

Because the physical characteristics of public housing — such as physical and geographical isolation, dense concentrations of residents, self containment, and few streets — may make these complexes convenient places to sell drugs, the residents become particularly vulnerable to the repercussions of drug activity. For example, if a resident or family member becomes a drug abuser, few resources are available for assistance; if drug dealers are highly visible, uniformed police have difficulty maintaining a presence in the area unless they are on foot; and although residents are fearful, economically they may be unable to move to different, more secure housing.

These same physical conditions in public housing make traditional policing methods — responding to 911 calls, surveillance, buy-bust, etc. — particularly ineffective against drug activity in these communities. Responding to 911 calls in these communities can be particularly fruitless. Police encounter unwilling or absent witnesses who fear retaliation, and face difficulties of physical access and lack of knowledge about the property. Officers, easily identifiable, often encounter fleet-footed and multiple dealers, and encounter elusive dealers being assisted, whether voluntarily or through coercion, by nearby residents.

If traditional policing methods don't work to resolve drug problems in public housing, what does work? That's a complex question and is best approached by identifying the distinct harms that drug dealing causes in low income neighborhoods.

Drug dealing in low income communities is manifested in several harms that impact both individuals and the neighborhood. These harms take shape in the following ways:

- violence
- corruption
- creation and support of criminal organizations
- disorder in public places such as vandalism, resulting in fear and loss of neighborhood morale
- physical harm to the users
- economic losses

- destructive effects upon youth population
- distrust of government and alienation from society

Each of these harms presents complex problems for police, PHAs, and residents of public housing, both for the short- and long-term. It is important to note that the degree of these harms varies from one community to the next, as do the ways in which these harms are manifested. There is little information available about the extent of these harms and what is available is not generalizable to all of the nation's public housing. Thus, cataloging the harms manifested in a specific community provides a useful mechanism for analyzing a community's drug problems — a first step in developing effective solutions for a specific neighborhood.

Violence

Violence and fear of violence are harmful to housing residents, housing officials and police. Indeed, the gratuitous violence related to drug activity has become the most important concern to residents in troubled communities. Because drug dealers are armed, even more than the actual abuse of drugs, residents are most concerned about "the aggressive gun-toting drug dealer" (Nadelmann, 1988: 18).

The armed drug dealers have indeed bred a new level of violence in some public housing complexes. Casualties include other retail level drug dealers who are killed or injured in turf battles; innocent bystanders who are caught in the crossfire of these turf battles; drug buyers who may get robbed or ripped off; fearful residents, who are intimidated into assisting the dealers or who become too frightened to venture outside their homes; and municipal and housing agency police (and their families), who must deal with the stress of the potentially violent conditions. Violence is not universal in public housing but it is a harmful condition prevalent in some of the more troubled public housing complexes.

Even though it may not be epidemic, the fear of violence is extremely high. Concern about violence ranked among the top three concerns of public housing residents in a survey of three public housing complexes in 1988. In Tampa, Atlanta and Tulsa, residents ranked violence nearly as big a problem in their community as drugs and crime.

Actual violent crime rates vary from one community to the next based on the economic status of the community. Violent crime is much higher in the underclass communities consisting of low income, minority residents. Homicides, rapes, aggravated assaults, and gunshot woundings feed these violent statistics (J. Wilson and DiIulio, 1989: 22-25). Some of the violence is directed within the family, and includes domestic abuse and child abuse by drug abusers.

Violence is also directed against the police and against PHA staff who, like the residents, learn to avoid trouble spots. Fear for personal safety becomes a rational response of PHA employees (including PHA security officers), police and residents.

Corruption

Another by-product of drug dealing that is harmful to poor communities is corruption. Corruption, when it exists or its appearance exists, harms the fragile bond between public housing residents and police or housing officials. This link, critical to handling drug problems, is a pervasive problem for both police and public housing agencies.

Police corruption. Both PHAs and police are susceptible to corruption linked with the illegal narcotic markets because the financial temptations to employees are enormous. Police officers conduct their work with little direct supervision and corruption is often difficult to detect. Police must come into close contact with those whom they areintended to control. This daily interaction with individuals who make their living from drug dealing and willingly pay a price to protect their livelihood increases the opportunity for police corruption.

Housing corruption. Similar employment conditions may also exist for housing personnel: little supervision, close contact with dealers, and large financial temptations. The temptation, in fact, may be stronger for housing personnel who often earn low wages, and whose corruption may also be difficult to detect. The notion of corruption of PHA personnel, however, is particularly important because housing staff may be able to learn of police actions and tip off dealers. In some complexes, residents and police have accused PHA employees of selling drugs. Some PHAs try to routinely monitor for such illegal behavior; other PHAs have difficulty scrutinizing employee behavior.

On the other hand, honest housing staff can offer valuable assistance to the police. In some complexes, PHA personnel routinely accompany police on drug busts. (One PHA security director said he would rather unlock the door for the police for a bust than have officers knock down the door.) In some complexes, PHA maintenance workers or inspectors routinely help police identify dealers or dwellings used for dealing.

Perceptions of corruption. More prevalent than corruption, perhaps, are the common perceptions by residents that police or housing officials are corrupt. The most frequently cited case is when police arrest a drug dealer who returns to the street within hours. That scene looks convincingly to area residents as if police are in league with the dealers. In fact, police may be putting arrestees into a criminal justice system which has exceeded its capacity.

In other cases, police may show up and residents are gone or no drugs are found indicating that the offenders were tipped off. These cases also affect the views of residents who see police or housing officials as either incompetent or corrupt. Both views are equally damaging to the relationship with residents.

The public's lack of understanding of police and housing administrative and legal processes can make above-board activities appear to be corrupt practices. Police and housing officials compound this misunderstanding when they do not take action against obvious drug problems. When officers daily drive past an apartment where drugs are sold and housing officials take no action to remove dealers from their units, residents may come to feel that the police and housing officials are on the take. In fact, policies and resource allocation procedures may tie the hands of officers and housing personnel.

Creation of Criminal Organizations

As drug-related crime has increased in the nation's large urban public housing complexes, so has the role of criminal organizations in some of these communities. These groups are business organizations, consisting of wholesale and retail outlets which market and distribute drugs. Their grip on the community can exceed their drug activity and can become a controlling force of everyday life in the community.

In terms of the nation's drug business, criminal drug dealing organizations are economic marketing units that operate drug activity as a business. These groups vary widely. There are major differences between regions, cities and in communities in terms of size, product sold,

54

sophistication, area of operation, and organizational structure.

A report by the United States Attorneys identified major drug organizations in the United States as consisting of (1) major international groups, such as Colombian cartel groups; (2) La Cosa Nostra and the Sicilian Mafia; (3) Asian organized crime groups, such as the Triads; (4) Jamaican posses; (5) outlaw motorcycle gangs; (6) California [or other local] street gangs; and (7) other domestic trafficking organizations (U.S. Justice Dept., 1989).

These last two groups seem to be more common in public housing although criminal organizations are not always easily identifiable. In Atlanta's public housing complexes, a group known as the "Miami Boys" was considered to have firm control of the drug trade. Police said this group of Florida-based suppliers would "often lure children from Atlanta's housing projects and other poor neighborhoods into selling the drugs on the streets or in crack houses." The group used children as sellers because they are not subjected to harsh adult legal penalties (Wells, 1988a).

In Chicago, street gangs preyed on the single women who predominate in public housing. Gang members would "use dwellings to store drugs and guns ... and convert buildings to private fortresses" by knocking out lights in elevators and stairwells, and cutting holes between apartments to elude rival gangs and police. The Disciples, Vice Lords and Cold Black were some of the dominant groups in Chicago's public housing complexes (Kotlowitz, 1988). In Philadelphia, the Junior Black Mafia was a major concern. In San Diego, several ethnic and neighborhood groups handled much of the city's drug trade.

Once these criminal drug-dealing organizations become established and entrenched in public housing, it becomes more difficult to impose criminal justice sanctions. Thus, greater difficulty is encountered in trying to wrest control of the community back from these formal criminal groups. However, it is important to note that formally organized gangs are not everywhere and there may be a tendency to see gangs where none exist.

In Tulsa, the local media carried a number of sensational stories describing the existence of gangs of West Coast origin in the Oklahoma city. Police investigations, however, revealed that the purported gangs consisted of only a few young males who wanted the status conferred by gang membership.

Disorder in Public Places

Another harm to the poor communities devastated by drug dealing and crime is the prevalence of public disorder in the community. A chief characteristic of this disorder is the pervasiveness of fear among residents and the loss of neighborhood morale (Kleiman and Putala, 1987: 2). As visible drug dealing increases, residents increasingly tend to avoid certain areas of the community, particularly at night. This withdrawal of informal social control of public areas contributes to the control of the neighborhood by the drug dealers.

Fear. In three public housing communities surveyed in 1988 (Tampa, Tulsa, and Atlanta), a majority of residents were extremely fearful. Up to 84 percent of residents said they were very worried about crime in their community. The most frequent response to avoiding trouble and crime in the community was to stay at home in the evening and nighttime hours. In Tulsa, 47 percent of respondents said they stayed home; in Atlanta, 73 percent; and, in Tampa, 88 percent (Allen, 1989; Huguley, 1989; Tampa Police Dept., 1989).

It is not uncommon in poor neighborhoods for residents to be fearful. Unlike middle class communities, residents in poor, minority communities are more likely to feel that crimes are being committed by their neighbors. Thus, residents in these areas are more likely to be suspicious and hostile toward each other, and more likely to perceive the police, rather than their neighbors, as the source of protection and security. These residents, however, are also less satisfied with police protection and less likely to believe their neighbors would summon the police if they saw a crime being committed (Greenberg, Rohe and Williams, 1983).

Fear of retaliation by drug dealers also has a major impact on residents, particularly in their willingness to talk to or call the police. Residents are apparently fearful that a call to 911 to report a crime will reveal their address to police, who may either intentionally or inadvertently reveal the caller's identity to watchful and vindictive dealers. Other residents, fearful of retaliation by drug dealers, refuse to even talk with officers who work in their community.

Thus, fear in poor communities, combined with the absence of social solidarity among neighbors, can contribute to increased loss of morale in the neighborhood and perpetuate disorder within the community.

Vandalism. Vandalism is a symptom of disorder within the low income community. Although vandalism is a problem for the police, it may be a low priority. Other, more serious, demands on police time usually take precedence.

But vandalism contributes to several problems within the poor housing community. It imposes substantial economic costs on the PHAs for maintenance. Acts of vandalism contribute to further vandalism, which increases the pace of deterioration. And the deterioration sends a signal about the community's attitudes to potential criminals. Thus, what might appear on the surface to be a trivial disorder problem has both serious implications and suggests responsibility for both PHAs and police. Vandalism in low income communities is a visible sign that neither the police nor PHAs care; or, if they do care, they are unable to handle the problem. The signs of vandalism also contribute to fear among residents.

Physical Harm to Users

The public housing neighborhoods ravaged by drug dealing are also fragile because drug users are unlikely to have the financial resources to bear the cost of their drug abuse. Hence, these costs, much more than in affluent neighborhoods, are more likely to be borne by the public. Those costs, for example, will be incurred by taxpayers funding public drug abuse programs or by non-users of drugs, such as accident or crime victims, who are individually harmed.

The physical harm of drug addiction is most vivid with the growing prevalence of crack babies, sometimes abandoned in public hospitals, who are born with multiple health problems including small size and drug addiction. These babies often require lengthy hospital stays at great cost.

Outpatient treatment programs are not widely available for drug abusers and are often not located within the poor areas. Inpatient treatment beds are extremely scarce. And treatment itself is uncertain, particularly when patients return to the same environment that once encouraged their drug use.

Economic Losses

Drug-dealing and drug-related crime drain the limited economic resources in public housing and deter expansion of business in the nearby areas. These economic losses hurt both individuals in the troubled public housing communities and the community itself.

First, there are economic losses which are imposed on individuals. This individual loss often occurs through property crime, as residents are often the victims of property crimes in their communities.

No one is certain what amount of property crime is associated with drug use. However, data from the National Institute of Justice reveals than a large percentage of arrestees in cities where research was conducted are under the influence of drugs. The numbers range from 85 percent in San Diego to 50 percent in Indianapolis. These figures haveimportant implications for determining the relationship between crime and drug use. Individuals may also be affected by the loss of economic opportunity in their neighborhoods in the form of foregone wages due to drug abuse, the absence of jobs or reduced employment opportunities.

Second, drug activity results in the loss of economic opportunity for some poor communities. Business expansion or entry is deferred because costs, particularly those related to security operations, are too high in the more troubled areas. Businesses also face a reduced labor pool, as new workers are unwilling to move to the area.

Third, the absence of economic opportunity may enhance the willingness of individuals to become involved in drug activity. Whether through choice or financial enticement, economic incentives to join the drug trade are present in troubled communities. Residents may be encouraged to let dealers use an apartment for drug use or sales, as a stash house or hiding place; youths may work for dealers as lookouts; and residents may themselves become dealers.

Each of these economic harms of drug activity tends to lock the poor community into a vicious cycle of dependence upon the drug-related economy. Thus, it is clear that the economic harms caused by drug activity result in longlasting problems in poor areas. These economic harms eventually serve only to strengthen the economic grip of drug dealers on the community.

Youth problems

Young people in poor communities are both particularly vulnerable to drug dealing and particularly harmed by its effects in their community. These harms take place on two levels. First, there are clear indications that drug abuse among youth is directly related to increased incidence of adolescent pregnancy. Drug abuse is also linked with poor grades in school and contributes to increased rates of dropping out from school and increases the likelihood of youth becoming involved with drug dealing (Jaynes and Williams, 1989: 413).

Second, youths in poor neighborhoods are especially vulnerable to the lure of drug dealers. These youths often perceive dealers as heroes or successful role models. Drug dealing also offers economic opportunity, albeit at the risk of criminal justice sanctions. For these youths, dealers are symbols of success when few other options exist. Furthermore, as penalties have increased for adult dealers, youths have often been recruited to sell drugs (Nadelmann, 1988: 18).

Youths come into the business as lookouts and may become a part, although a dispensable part, of the drug-dealing operation. Once youths get involved in the drug trade, they are more likely to be caught and subjected to punishment for their criminal behavior. Arrest rates are high for black youths. For example, Tulsa, OK, reported a 736 percent increase in the incidence of drug arrests for black male youths in a ten-year period. The arrests of white youths dropped 5 percent in the same period (Allen, 1989).

Because of higher arrest rates, black juveniles are being increasingly subjected to punishment for their behavior. Criminal behavior and its punishment consequently pose significant barriers to educational excellence and to employment for black youth, perpetuating a cycle of economic barriers. When this punishment takes black males out of the community, the absence of husbands, fathers, and positive role models becomes a further problem in the community. An important effect of the high black crimes rates is the perpetuation of negative stereotypes and fears of blacks, especially fears of young males (Jaynes and Williams, 1989: 498).

In these ways, the dynamics of drug activity causes severe and longlasting harm to the youth in the nation's poor communities. The drama of this ruthless cycle is played out in many public housing communities.

Distrust of Government

Drug dealing that persists in a community for long periods of time causes significant harm to the community's relationship with public and private agencies. Drug activity in poor communities can be manifested in antagonism from citizens towards both police and PHAs. Residents who feel neglected or abandoned, stereotyped or mistreated, develop a distrust for government that is heightened by racial differences. This distrust serves to further alienate public housing residents from the rest of the city.

Consequently, both police and public housing agencies often face outright hostility from the very citizens they try to serve in low income communities.

That antagonism makes the jobs of both organizations more difficult.

Research has shown that bureaucratic procedures in poor communities often produce "indifference, suspicion or outright hostility" (Greenberg, Rohe and Williams, 1983: 7). Some housing officials and police have tried to be less bureaucratic and involve residents in developing and implementing solutions to neighborhood problems. These measures have met varying degrees of success. Indeed, black residents in urban areas were found to be "less satisfied with police protection," but this group was also more likely to rely on police for protection (Greenberg, Rohe and Williams, 1983: 6). The finding suggests a dilemma for police and housing officials who want community involvement in solving drug problems.

When antagonism persists between police and residents, the problems are increased. "Bad community feelings do more than simply create tensions — they engender actions against the police that may embitter police and trigger irrational responses from them. Citizens, in turn, become more hostile toward police. Because of the absence of public support, police become less effective and crime is stimulated. In other words, police fail not only to prevent crime but may inadvertently encourage its rise" (Skolnick and Bayley, 1988: 41).

That hostility can be visible when police enter low income communities. In Tulsa, OK, officers voiced concern about crowds gathering in the low income communities. In Atlanta, GA, crowds in public housing on occasion became hostile, and resorted to rock and bottle throwing and chanted "police brutality" as officers made arrests. These actions are symptoms of deeper problems within the community.

Lack of a good community relationship affects the police in other ways. In some communities, residents hesitate to call for service, because they believe the police will not respond. In other communities, citizens may call with false or inflated reports. Lack of good community relations also means police get little input from witnesses and little useful information from citizens about illicit activity.

The Impact of Harms

That drug dealing harms law-abiding citizens is no surprise to police officials or housing personnel. But exactly how citizens are harmed is worth evaluating for it is at this level that the community can become involved in solving its problems, that is, by reducing the harms being suffered.

Each of the harms identified in this section has important implications for the police.

- Violence creates fear among police, housing officials and residents
- Corruption suggests specific police and housing responses, such as mandatory drug testing, increased supervision and other anti-corruption measures
- Criminal organizations can supercede police authority and run public housing complexes
- Loss of neighborhood morale increases a community's reliance upon police service, rather than the community assuming a portion of this role
- Physical harm to the users results in economic costs borne by the public
- Economic losses include property crimes committed by drug abusers stimulating demand for police service

- Drug activity lures youths into illegal activity
- Distrust of government means residents don't cooperate with the police

Since these effects of drug dealing that harm the public housing community have such a direct impact on police and increase the demand for police service, it is a logical step to address these harms in designing a police response to community drug-related problems. These harms in fact create a common agenda to unite police, public housing and residents in pursuing a mutual goal.

What Can Be Done?

What if drug problems in public housing are too severe for police to resolve? One police option for dealing with persistent drug problems may be to recognize that the problems are too deep and the area is too far gone to invest any more effort.

Indeed, one author, acknowledging the difficulty of policing hard core drug areas, said: "It is hard to imagine the police being able to do more than drive the dealing back into the public-housing projects and other relatively small areas in which the police are unable to maintain a presence" (Kaplan, 1988: 45).

The perception that police have given up on communities deeply troubled by drug problems has given rise to the feeling that police don't care about public housing and the people who live there. One HUD official commented that police treat public housing as if it were a separate country.

Police agencies are often accused of being concerned about drug and crime problems only when they spill out of poor areas and into middle class communities — the separate country treatment. In fact, some citizens believe police make a concerted effort to contain drug problems within low income communities.

The reality is that police deployment or calls for service may be higher in these troubled areas. Some police agencies have assigned foot patrols to public housing, opened mini-stations within the complexes, or developed other strategies which counter the notion of police avoidance of public housing problems. However, the police response to these problems varies widely around the country.

If police do give up on public housing communities and residents, the repercussions are likely to be longlasting. In the event that problems are ignored or deferred within public housing communities, problems will only increase within those communities, adjacent neighborhoods and the entire city. Consider these remarks from a court-appointed receiver for the Boston Housing Authority: "Ultimately, the withdrawal of institutional supports destroys any sense of cooperative capacity among residents, destroys any sense of community. Each family becomes an isolated fearful unit. Poverty has already impressed on them a sense of powerlessness — now the violence that consumes the community and frightens and humiliates them daily gives final proof of their impotence" (Boston Housing Authority, 1988).

That sense of dislocation has implications for the police effort. Indeed, rather than containing drug problems in these areas, special attention should be given to drug sales in poor neighborhoods because poor neighborhoods are particularly fragile and their residents are particularly vulnerable to the ill effects of drug dealing (Kleiman and Putala, 1987). So it is clear that "writing off" troubled communities won't solve any problems and is likely to escalate problems in the community.

Another option that police have for dealing with drug-burdened communities is to strengthen law enforcement efforts, that is, to increase arrests. However, the reality is that in many cities, the criminal justice system is not much of a deterrent to drug activity because of the overcrowded facilities. For example, in Philadelphia, despite increases in arrests, court records show that few drug offenders are actually convicted. Those who are convicted seldom serve any substantial prison time. Instead of active time, most drug offenders are placed on probation (Meeks and Hasson, 1989: xvii). Many other cities also face jail moratoriums and occupancy problems.

Thus, it becomes clear that if criminal justice sanctions aren't the answer, a potential strategy is for police to address the harms caused by drug activity in the community.

What does it mean for police to address harms in the community? It means developing and implementing strategies that focus on the specific ways in which drug activity harms the community rather than addressing the dealing itself. This is a subtle but important distinction in the way goals are defined. The objective of addressing harms is not to eliminate drug dealing per se, which may in fact be beyond police capabilities. Instead, the objective of addressing harms is to reduce the harms caused to the community by the persistent drug activity. This objective creates a common agenda for police, PHAs and residents. Thus, addressing harms also means linking up the police with a pair of uncommon allies — in this case, PHAs and public housing residents, the two other actors with the greatest stake in resolving or reducing harm in the public housing community.

PHAs may seem an unlikely ally for urban police agencies. However, PHAs and police departments share some common organizational issues which drive the way in which they do business. In urban areas with dwindling tax bases, many police departments have faced limited financial resources reminiscent of the scarce resources which became a way of life for PHAs during the 1970s.

Both PHAs and police agencies are bureaucracies and this organizational structure can slow the implementation of innovative responses to problems. By working together, however, personnel from both agencies may be able to develop cooperative efforts and become more responsive to community needs.

Both PHAs and police agencies also face rigorous public review of their actions; the public has demanded a certain level of accountability; and the legal system is often invoked as a review mechanism for policies, procedures and actions of both PHAs and police. Thus, in many ways, the police and public housing share some common organizational characteristics. Having these characteristics in common and recognizing these characteristics as possible barriers can aid the relationship between PHA and police.

By defining a common agenda to tackle drug problems — by focusing on the harms of drug activity — PHAs, police and public housing residents have an opportunity to develop and implement a collaborative effort to resolve drug problems at the community level. This chapter has suggested an agenda for developing that collaborative relationship. The next chapter describes a process for developing and implementing a collaborative effort.

V.

Developing a Relationship

It is worthwhile for local police to invest the time to develop a relationship with their public housing authority and with public housing residents. Although little is known about the actual characteristics that make one housing complex a hotbed of trouble, while another complex a block away may be trouble free, joint efforts between agencies have the potential to solve problems that neither can handle on its own (Bratt, 1986: 356).

Developing a relationship with PHA personnel and public housing residents also involves sharing with key housing players information about the role of the police. Many citizens and police persist in their belief that the police function is solely to regulate the conduct of individuals by invoking the criminal justice system. The contemporary view, however, is that police have a broader role than solely the enforcement of laws. Instead of only a crime-fighter role, the police objective is to solve problems that cause harm or have the potential to cause harm to citizens. If housing officials and residents judge police solely upon number of arrests and response time, they may find the police response to problems wanting. However, if joint goals are established to reduce harms, such as cleaning up a perennial trouble spot, everyone can participate in resolving the problem and results can be measured with the same yardstick.

Police should also communicate to housing officials and residents that police are trying to work with them to solve their problems in a systematic way. The express support from key executives is important at this stage. The city's mayor or manager, police commissioner or chief, and housing executive director should be in agreement on this issue. This message can be communicated through key police policies if problem-oriented policing has been adopted as an organizational goal. For example, the Philadelphia Police Department's mission statement reads: "The mission of the Philadelphia Police Department is to work in a true partnership with our fellow citizens of Philadelphia: to enhance the quality of life in our city, and by raising the level of public safety through law enforcement to reduce the fear and incidence of crime." The elements of "quality of life," "partnership" and "fear of crime" are important components in this mission statement. If the police department is committed to these objectives, they should be expressed clearly to housing personnel and residents. A written policy is a good start but citizens and housing officials will want evidence of the practical application of this policy.

Of course, for residents and housing officials to believe this philosophy, police executives, managers, supervisors and officers must all be firmly committed to the objectives. The officers who work with the PHA must also accept the notion that police can and should take an active role in identifying specific community problems (which are not always or only crime problems) and bringing public and private resources together to solve or ease problems. (This concept has been fully addressed in Herman Goldstein's, **Problem-Oriented Policing** and **Problem Solving** by John Eck and William Spelman.) Officers and police managers must recognize that any police strategy that relies exclusively on motorized patrol, responding quickly to calls for service, and investigating crimes after the fact will do little to solve a community's problems or reduce fearfulness (Moore and Trojanowicz, 1988: 6). That reality is amplified in low income neighborhoods where these traditional policing strategies have produced few long-term impacts, particularly for drug-related problems.

Because public housing communities are predominantly minority, police must also confront the reality of prejudice by race and class held by some officers. Human relations training for officers may help them be more sensitive to deeply-rooted racial or class prejudices, or aware of cultural differences in some communities. Clear and enforced policies should be in place in every police agency to prevent prejudice from being acted out. Procedures should be established to elicit feedback from residents: Do residents feel as if they are being treated fairly by police? One way to get an answer to this question is to ask residents directly. Other opportunities for feedback occur at community meetings.

A perennial question in police agencies is whether only minority officers should be assigned to work in predominantly minority neighborhoods. A number of departments have concluded that all of their officers should be able to work in any part of the jurisdiction and that assignments should take place without regard to race or socioeconomic characteristics.

Some practical questions come into play on this issue. If police are working in a minority community that does not speak English, such as an Asian or Hispanic community, officers with these language skills will need to be available or assigned. Likewise, undercover officers may need to reflect the common demographic characteristics of an area where they are working. If only blacks buy drugs in a particular spot, it makes little sense to send in a white officer undercover.

Police administrators, however, should carefully avoid stereotyping their officers, for example, by assigning only black officers to black communities. Likewise, administrators should not assume that black officers will be any more knowledgeable about public housing areas than white.

If the police are committed to establishing a relationship with public housing, the first battle may be to overcome skepticism on the part of PHA management and residents. Many public housing residents have jaundiced views of the police, some of which are based on actual experience. Memories of earlier eras of racial injustice or physical abuse by officers are heavy emotional baggage for residents. In some cases, skepticism can be overcome only with persistence by the officers in demonstrating a true commitment to easing the problems in these low income neighborhoods. In some cases, residents may be more supportive than PHA management; in other cases, the opposite situation may prevail.

It was mentioned earlier that poor minority residents tend to look towards police, rather than neighbors, for protection. This finding, however, should not imply that poor minority residents trust the police. Research has shown that lack of trust and suspicion of mostly white organizations and their intentions is a prevalent attitude among minorities (Jaynes and Williams, 1989: 131). Clearly, developing a trusting relationship is likely to take a lot of work and patience on the part of police.

Thus, in developing a cooperative relationship between police and public housing, a preliminary step should include an honest assessment of the police agency. Questions to be asked include: Does the police organization fully support developing collaborative relationships? Is the agency sensitive, in policy and practice, to the needs of the public housing community? Do officers need assistance, experience or training to ensure sensitivity to minority needs?

Developing a Plan of Action

Once the police agency has committed itself to tackling drug-related problems in public housing, officers and managers detailed to the effort should develop a plan of action to ensure the most efficient use of their resources and that a comprehensive approach is used. That game plan should include several key steps which are covered in this chapter.

The plan for the strategy is an analytical approach which involves identifying the problem, analyzing the problem, responding to the problem, and then assessing the progress made in resolving the problem. Several key steps can be used to guide the efforts.

First, the police agency should engage in a process to rigorously and carefully identify the precise problem which is to be addressed. This is a deceivingly complex process because the problem should be viewed not only from the perspective of the police, but also from the perspective of public housing residents and the housing agency as well. Information must be collected that verifies exactly what the problem is. Since drug activity harms different groups and individuals, it should be determined exactly who is being harmed by the problem in a specific community and how these people are being harmed? Second, police must develop a collaborative relationship with the housing agency and residents (and other groups which have a stake in the community) to develop a strategy that can use all the resources available. Learning about these groups is a good start.

Third, a strategy must be developed and implemented which is determined to fit the needs of those affected by the problem. Finally, an important

Key Steps in Solving Problems in Public Housing

A. Fact-Finding Mission
   1) Identify key players
   2) Learn about each organization
   3) Determine what programs are in place, and level of participation
B. Preliminary Identification and Analysis of Problem
   1) What is the problem and for whom? Police, residents, housing personnel, mayor, etc.
   2) What information verifies there is a problem and how severe is the problem?
   3) Does one problem mask another problem?
C. Develop a Dialogue with Key Players
   1) Bring everyone abreast of progress
   2) Enlist support, mobilize community
   3) Assess resources, build a coalition
D. Develop a Strategy
   1) Collect more information if necessary
   2) Refine problem definition with input from coalition
   3) Develop goals and objectives
   4) Review what strategies and tactics are being used elsewhere
E. Select and Implement a Response
   1) Coordinate a response with all available resources
   2) Specify roles for each player
   3) Determine time frame
   4) Tap other resources, such as schools, utilities, social services
   5) Determine appropriate measures for success
F. Evaluate Progress
   1) Was the problem improved or changed?
   2) Redefine objectives

step is to document the progress that was made in the effort. The following section of this monograph reviews each of these steps in depth.

Fact-Finding Mission

An integral component of developing a relationship with housing is getting to know the key players of the PHA — members of the board of directors, executive director, managers, the head of security, and other staff members. First, identify which individuals serve in these roles. Then identify an appropriate forum for meeting these people. It may be on an individual basis, such as making an appointment to meet them in their office. A regularly scheduled meeting, such as a Neighborhood Watch, or other gathering may also be a good occasion for officers to meet these housing officials.

Residents, individually and through tenant councils, are also important actors in the operation of the properties of the housing authority. It should be a high priority to meet these people. Tenant councils often meet on a regular basis; non-participating residents may be met through a door-to-door approach or at other neighborhood meetings, at schools or churches. Police can also become familiar with residents by spending time in the community. Obviously, that time commitment must extend beyond driving through the community or arriving on the scene only to make arrests.

Each housing interest group — both residents and housing personnel — has a different but critical role in the operation of housing policies. Each group is important in developing a cooperative relationship with police and establishing goals.

Collecting information about the PHA as an organization is both useful and necessary in any police effort to tackle problems in public housing. The PHA is a key player and officers should become familiar with the organization and the processes which frame its operations. For example, police should obtain a copy of the PHA lease, which defines the relationship between the PHA and residents. As with the private sector, leases define the rules and obligations with which tenants must comply to continue living in the dwelling. Leases can be modified; in fact, a number of PHAs have recently incorporated clauses specifying that illegal substances *found* in units is just cause for eviction.

Police can collect other information about the PHA through published policies including the housing agency's grievance procedure for tenants, tenant screening criteria, and other documents. Police can attend regular meetings of the PHA board of commissioners, which are open to the public.

Officers can also seek out invitations to attend tenant council meetings. At meetings of this sort, officers may identify residents who are supportive of the police role in the community. Despite common views that criminals proliferate in public housing, most of the tenants are in fact law-abiding citizens who are willing to provide assistance to officers if their anonymity can be assured.

These meetings are also an opportunity to begin building a relationship, sharing information about the police initiative in public housing, and developing a framework for action. Police should also be alert so they can identify existing leaders and patterns of leadership among residents, and learn of any other residents who may be excluded from this group. Building a coalition with residents may mean dealing with political cliques already in existence, or developing new groups. At this delicate stage of the process, officers should be careful to avoid taking sides, or being perceived as taking sides. It is not uncommon for there to be internal disputes among residents. Again, at this stage, police should invest time only in collecting information such as identifying potential problems among competing groups.

While obtaining formal information about the operations of the PHA from written policies, officers should also seek to gain informal information about practices. Sometimes policy and practice may differ widely. For example, a PHA may have a policy of evicting anyone convicted of selling illegal drugs. In practice, however, how do housing officials get that information, and how quickly do they evict the offender? Informal information about practices may provide great insight into organizations, especially their day-to-day operations. On occasion, such information can provide clues for building an information network, and building a coalition to support implementing responses to problems once those responses are formulated.

In working with PHAs, police should carefully avoid telling the PHA how to conduct its business or making judgments about the organization. The search for information may reveal inadequacies in management. Unless there are possible violations of the law, police should largely accept these conditions as a state of reality with which police must deal. Indeed, any organizational inadequacies are elements which police must consider in developing responses. Discovering those weaknesses is part of the fact-finding mission.

Corruption, however, is a separate issue. On occasion, police may suspect housing officials or employees of being involved with drug activity, either selling drugs or shielding drug activity. A common suspicion is that drug dealers are tipped off before police arrive for a raid. An officer who suspects corruption should not ignore it. There is an Inspector General for the HUD office in Washington, D.C., which investigates corruption. Suspicion of corruption should be reported to the PHA or regional HUD office.

Police should collect a great deal of other information about the public housing organization. For example, if the authority has a security force, it is useful to find out exactly what role this force plays in the day-to-day operations of the properties. Is the security force armed? Does this security staff have powers of arrest? Does the security force engage in evictions, or monitor ingress to buildings? How does security view its relationship with police? Again, it is useful to collect information about the formal role of the security force. The role of the security force may be recorded on paper in a formal policy but officers should also gather informal information about how the security force works. Find out through conversations with other PHA personnel or residents what the security division does and how, not just its written role. In many cases, actual performance may differ from projections and expectations.

Security operations are a key topic for which police should gather careful information. Other key areas include admissions and evictions, maintenance and administration/operations. Police, for example, need to know who lives in a target public housing complex. Are occupants primarily families or senior citizens? How large is the youth population? What screening criteria does the PHA use for admission? What priorities for admission are considered, such as, are homeless persons given priority over other applicants?

How often are residents evicted? What conditions must exist before an eviction takes place? How long does an eviction take? What grievance practice is followed?

How quickly are units turned over or re-rented? How many units are vacant? How does the PHA monitor for abandoned units? Is the policy to board up units? How quickly is this done and what materials are used? Does the PHA suffer from vandalism problems? What kind of problems occur and where in the community?

On an administrative level, what social service or other programs does the PHA offer to residents? Are tenants involved in management and towhat extent?

These are the kinds of questions that provide useful information to police. However, officers should be careful not to be overly judgmental while collecting information. Most PHAs have scarce resources, and many PHAs are barely able to survive economically. Many PHA employees give their jobs their best effort but have been demoralized over the years because of scarce resources and pressure from the many masters who control the operations of the PHA. And, like police departments, PHAs are part of a large bureaucracy which operate with written rules and policies, and are sometimes slow to change. Employees usually learn to work within that structure, and may sometimes bend the rules to accomplish what they view as a worthwhile objective.

While collecting information, officers should also look within the police organization. In many cities, police powers on PHA property are greater than on other privately-owned property. Officers should explore whether police are formally designated as agents of the housing authority, or have other powers which permit wider latitude in police action, such as enforcing trespassing ordinances and so forth.

Since cities operate under cooperative agreements with PHAs, police may want to review these documents to determine the precise obligation of the police agency to public housing. This document may provide a starting point for developing a more productive relationship.

Preliminary Problem Identification

Once police have collected basic information that provides a framework for understanding the environment in which they will be focusing their efforts, it is important to develop a preliminary identification of the problem. Identifying problems — manageable, narrow problems within thehousing complex — is the first goal of the officer's effort to solve the problems. Both police and housing personnel and residents should recognize that the "drug problem" in low income housing is composed of a variety of smaller problems. The goal of the effort should be to tackle manageable problems that can realistically be attacked.

Thus, officers must be more specific than saying the problem in the public housing complexes is "drugs." "The drug problem" in its entirety sounds far too difficult to tackle and implies unrealistic goals — such as totally eliminating the use of illegal drugs — that may be impossible to achieve. So officers must carefully frame their definition of the problem. For example, if the problem is viewed as related to drugs, is it a problem with street-level dealing of crack cocaine by 14- and 15-year old male youths who are truant from school? Or is the problem that many residents are abusing drugs and thus unable to pay their rent, hold jobs or supervise their children? Or is the problem that violence (assaults and shootings) associated with disputes between competing dealers creates a fearful environment for residents who live nearby?

Is the problem that residents are selling drugs from their homes? If so, can it be determined which homes and which residents are involved? Have there been any arrests? Who are the buyers? Do these buyers come from a certain part of the city? Are the sellers the leaseholders for the units, or are the sellers "sub-

80

leasing" apartments with money or through intimidation, sex, or drugs? If the problem is a combination of these problems, it is still important to identify each component

In identifying the specific drug-related problems to be tackled in low income housing, it is useful to learn about the housing authority's and residents' perception of the problem. These individuals may view their community's problem quite differently from the police. In developing a response, the viewpoint of each affected community must be considered.

For example, the Chicago PHA at one point denied any knowledge of gang activity in their dwelling units. But police and tenants had firsthand knowledge of occupation by a ruthless and violent gang (Kotlowitz, 1988). The PHA executive director later reporting that drug activity "was tightly controlled by highly organized gangs..." The comments followed on the heels of a cooperative law enforcement-housing intervention in drug activity. It would have been difficult to develop such a collaborative relationship and approach unless varying viewpoints were aired and resolved.

Residents can be a rich source of information. Surveying a sample of residents can provide information about specific drug-related problems and produce a bonus benefit of developing a relationship between police and residents. Residents live in these complexes 24 hours a day — they know who deals drugs, where, and how. If tapped, residents are the best source of information available to the police because they are also the most directly harmed by drug activity.

In tackling a drug problem, it is likely that each actor — police, housing officials, and residents — may have a different priority for the element of the drug problem which they find most troubling, that is, most harmful. Yet the priorities of these actors may be closely linked.

For example, the PHA may view the worst problem as the graffiti and vandalism which seem to accompany drug dealing. Police may view the problem as excessive number of low priority calls for service. The biggest concern of residents may be their fear of going outside their apartments. These concerns can be crafted into a goal that meets everyone's needs. For example, the visual impact of the vandalism may contribute to the fear which residents have; residents may call police excessively because they're afraid. Thus, a cooperative anti-vandalism program could work to reduce maintenance costs for the PHA, restore feelings of safety among residents, and reduce calls for service.

Develop a Dialogue with Key Players

Once a problem is identified, the police should make every effort to ensure that key actors become involved in the effort to tackle the problems. Perhaps the most important accomplishment police can make is to mobilize the community around a jointly-defined problem.

Tenant involvement is absolutely critical. HUD notes that security problems in public housing often are more difficult when "residents are disorganized and isolated from one another" (Kolodny, Baron and Struyk, 1983a: 90). In fact, developing a plan of action without input and cooperation from residents is likely, at best, to produce only short-term results or no results at all. "How else can effective crime prevention programs be developed *without* community involvement?" asked one community organizer who advocates a collaborative approach to community crime problems (Misner, 1973: 44). Thus, police who have conducted street sweeps in poor communities without working with the community to leave a support system in place for the law-abiding residents, have found the results of their efforts fleeting. In other sweep efforts where residents have not been included, residents have been angry or resentful about the police activity.

Experiments in developing collaborative relationships between police and the community affected by drug problems have shown great promise. In Oxnard, CA, police developed a network within the community to aid them in resolving an enduring drug problem at a specific location. Residents provided information, monitored the problem, and provided valuable assistance to resolving the problem.

In some Tulsa, OK, public housing complexes, foot patrol officers have gotten to know residents by sight and name. Thus, when officers see a stranger in the area, they conduct a field interview and require the name of the person being visited, or proof of residence. Trespassing laws are firmly enforced, and residents regularly give officers information about any illegal activity.

Indeed, HUD suggests that residents, when mobilized, build "feelings of solidarity and mutual aid" which can "play an important role in helping to alleviate fear of crime where it is exaggerated beyond its true dimensions" (Kolodny, Baron and Struyk, 1983a: 90).

Perhaps the biggest hurdle for officers to overcome in attempting to mobilize a public housing community is dealing with the issue of apathy among residents. Mobilizing the community is a big challenge. Because of enduring patterns of being isolated from the rest of the city, including the police, poor residents are often slow to develop trust and get involved.

One perception of police success in poor neighborhoods is that police must first "regain" control of the streets from drug dealers, then turn control of the streets over to the community. These strategies are alternately known as community empowerment, community policing, coproduction and similar names. The basic idea, however, is that once police show "control," then effective relationships with the community can be established. That is the approach which Inspector Edward J. McLaughlin of Philadelphia's South Police Division calls "stabilizing the neighborhood." This is a process through which police, who may have once retreated from the problems, can reassert their influence in the troubled community, often through traditional measures such as increased patrol and increased arrests.

It is at this point following stabilization that police may meet a positive response from the citizens in the community. In trying to rebuild a sense of community which can take an active role in deterring crime such as overt street dealing, police should call upon the active involvement of citizens. The police role should not be to decide the priorities and responsibilities of the community, but to encourage the residents to develop such a plan.

. However, police may very well encounter failure as they try to build such a consensus. The option for police at this point is to recognize the difficulty of the task, identify barriers to mobilizing the community, and try again. Surveys indicate that residents have strong concerns about crime and drugs in their community and are fearful for themselves and their children. If police can tap these emotions and channel them into positive actions, it is possible that substantive progress can be achieved.

There is a possibility that community groups and other organizations with which police can work are already in place. Thus, it is important during this phase of the public housing-police initiative, that police conduct a resource assessment to determine every agency or organization which is involved with public housing and learn about the programs or resources those organizations offer or can make available.

These organizations largely fall into some convenient groupings for issues related to public housing, and particularly to drugs and public housing initiatives. Consider assessing resources within the following framework:

Treatment Sources/Programs
    Hospitals and clinics, public and private
    Health Department
    Narcotics Anonymous and similar programs
    Mental Health agencies

Prevention/Education
    Schools and universities
    Media
    Crime prevention programs
    Libraries

Criminal Justice System
    Other Law Enforcement Agencies
    Courts
    Prosecutors
    Corrections

Other Public Agencies
    Code Enforcement
    Public Works
    Public Utilities
    Social Services
    Parks and Recreation
    Housing Agency
    Legislatures (city, county or state)
    Transportation services
    Planning agencies

Fire Department
Tax offices
Utilities

Community Organizations
Neighborhood Watch
Churches
Job Corps
Scouting programs
TipLines
Civic groups
Charitable groups
Social service organizations

This is only a partial list of organizations which may be involved or have an interest in an initiative to tackle drug problems in public housing. Other groups may well come to mind, such as private sector organizations including banks, insurance companies, contract services whomay work in the area (such as garbage collection), and other private companies (for example, telephone companies who may service phones in the area). The list of possible resources should be fully explored.

Once all the resources have been identified and their contributions determined, a useful goal is to build a coalition of everyone who is affected by the problem or can make a contribution to easing the problem.

Develop a Strategy

Developing a response tailored to the individual community is a process that requires creativity and imagination.

Consider, first, redefining the problem to ensure that the problem definition is appropriate for everyone involved and that everyone can buy into or agree on the goals established. For example, on some occasions, police may address the problem from only the police perspective and not be able to empathize with residents and see the harms to individuals in the community. In Newport News, VA, officers decided to tackle a burglary problem which existed in a low income community. After collecting a great deal of information about the problem (including valuable information from residents), officers realized the real problem wasn't burglaries; instead, the real problem was the physical inadequacy of the pre-World War II buildings. The biggest concern of residents was the physical structure of the buildings, and it became clear that the deterioration and shoddy structures contributed to the problem of burglaries.

In other cases, those individuals or groups directly affected by a problem may not be able to see the forest for the trees. A resident may only be concerned about drug dealing in an adjacent residence or a particular individual, when in fact that dealing is part of an area-wide dealing problem perhaps linked with truancy or insufficient employment opportunities. Again, redefining the problem is an important step to crafting a response. A key to effective problem-solving efforts is to look creatively at the information gathered about the problem to determine an effective response, that is, to find a unique way to intervene.

There are many examples of creative strategies being crafted to meet local needs. One example of an unusual intervention is an approach taken in Omaha, NE, public housing. Because youths were involved in street level drug dealing, housing officials crafted a program that rewards youths for remaining in school. School attendance and scholastic achievement earn awards, tutoring services are available, and, if parents fail to keep their children in school, the family can be evicted. Police may be able to work with housing officials to develop similar responses (U.S. HUD, 1989a).

In Tacoma, WA, police, frustrated by their inability to establish probable cause when drug deals were obviously taking place on street corners, got the local city council to enact a specific ordinance. The ordinance allowed police to make arrests of individuals appearing to engage in drug-related activity in known drug dealing locations. Spotting known drug dealing mannerisms was one element for an arrest. Other cities have adopted similar anti-loitering ordinances.

One useful way to review strategies that may be available to the police initiative is to categorize strategies in terms of desired outcomes or goals. For example, in Omaha, the organizational goal was to prevent youths from becoming involved in drug-related activity. In Tacoma, the explicit outcome desired was to remove offenders from specific areas.

There are five general categories of responses which provide a framework for crafting a strategy tailored to a specific geographic area:

- **Improve the physical environment.** In an effort to restore a sense of order to drug-ravaged communities, the physical environment is often considered the primary visual clue to disorder. Improving lighting, fencing, access and other physical conditions is part of this desired outcome.

- **Remove offenders.** Removing offenders from specific areas often means invoking the criminal justice system, for example, making arrests. But a number of other strategies can be used to get drug dealers away from certain areas, including evicting residents of public housing who engage in drug dealing or harbor drug traffickers.

- **Reduce demand.** Efforts that focus on deterring
  people from using or buying drugs, including
  reverse buys and prevention or treatment
  referrals, all come under the category of
  reducing demand. Many police agencies get
  involved in educational programs, such as
  DARE (Drug Abuse Resistance Education).

- **Improve intelligence.** A number of police
  agencies have focused their efforts on improving
  the information they can tap about drug
  problems. These responses focus on activities
  such as installing drug tip lines, developing
  informant networks, getting information from
  residents — all designed to improve the
  information of police.

- **Empower residents.** In some areas, police and
  other organizations have focused on the deeper
  social problems that may exist in drug-ravaged
  communities. Empowering residents means
  helping needy people get the tools they need to
  have a better life. Empowerment strategies may
  include making telephones accessible (for police
  calls and other needs), developing access to
  transportation so the individuals can get to jobs
  and interviews, tapping community resources to
  provide day care and other needed services,
  providing positive role models for youths in the
  community, or helping to build self-esteem
  among people who have little. Police are often
  involved not in the delivery of these programs
  but in accessing and linking needs with useful

information and resources.

There are many different alternatives for action available for police. Looking at responses within this goal-based framework provides an organization a context for selecting appropriate responses. This framework will be used in the next chapter to describe some efforts of police to deal with drug problems in public housing. It is extremely useful to consider what other police agencies and other cities with similar problems are doing, take the best and the most appropriate ideas and adapt them as necessary.

But it is equally important not to try a wholesale transplant of another city's or law enforcement agency's response to a problem. If problems have been identified in a manageable way for a specific neighborhood, they may appear similar to another city. But communities are different, with different histories and individuals, and different patterns of problems. Just as doctors must do research and typing of blood and other vital body fluids of host and source before transplanting organs, police must research the strategies and determine which ones may work best. Resources also vary from community to community, as do the interest and willingness of residents or other organized groups to become involved, and the city's or area's history and relationship with police and other groups. All these variations must be considered. Even after a strategy is selected, police will need to nurture the implementation, and fine tune the strategy to ensure that it is working as intended.

Select and Implement a Response

A wide range of strategies will have been considered in developing a response. It is important not to reject those that may seem offbeat or difficult to implement. For example, in Baltimore County, MD, officers routinely brainstorm in groups and sometimes come up with unusual but effective responses to problems. Similarly, traditional law enforcement strategies should be neither rejected nor relied upon as the sole strategy in responding to community problems. The effective response is likely to include several different strategies rather than just one and law enforcement can be a key part of that response.

Once a response is selected, it must be implemented. Implementation involves a number of different components ranging from personnel allocation to budgeting.

Some of the components that should be considered and resolved prior to implementation include:

- **Response selection.** The strategies included in the response should be clearly identified and agreed upon by participating agencies.

- **Scheduling.** Determine where, when, how, who. These questions are especially important if the department has rotating shifts or has variation in assignments. The "who" question will also include individuals and agencies outside the police agency. Beginning and ending dates also should be determined.

- **Roles and responsibilities.** The role and responsibility of each organization and individual involved in the implementation should be defined, again including those both within and outside the police agency.

- **Funding.** Budget issues should be considered and resolved, particularly if overtime or additional funds will be necessary for police personnel.

- **Communication.** The response plan will need to be communicated (perhaps marketed) to other collaborating agencies, and other departments within the police agency (such as narcotics). The police chief and other police personnel may need to sign off on the plan. The media may need to be informed or a process planned for doing so after the response goes into effect.

- **Training.** Police or other agency personnel may need exposure to some training to enable them to implement the response. This training, for example, could include exposure to the operations of cooperating agencies, such as housing authorities, resident councils, or other groups. The cooperating agencies may need to learn about police procedures, such as probable cause or requirements for search warrants.

- **Anticipating results.** The architects of the response should define the results anticipated. Unanticipated results that may occur should also be considered as well as negative repercussions to the response. This step of response implementation should also include a Plan B, that is, what to do if Plan A does not work as anticipated, and when Plan B should be implemented.

- **Evaluation planning.** The measures to assess the effectiveness of the response should be identified prior to implementation so that data collection measures can be put in place. Several measures should be identified because these multiple gauges will insure that successes (or failures) are documented. This documentation is a great tool for convincing the chain of command to expand the response, or may indicate why the current response should be abandoned or modified.

Each of these components of implementing a response should be considered for a complex response. Some responses may be simple and have few elements; others will be more complex.

An example of the intricacies of implementing a collaborative response was apparent in Chicago's Clean Sweep operation. In that response, police and housing officials worked together to launch an effort which was designed to control access to public housing buildings. Housing and police had long recognized that there was a severe problem related to drug-dealing and violence in the public housing communities. However, learning that 80 percent of the crimes were being committed by unauthorized residents or non-residents prompted housing and police officials to focus on an access control goal.

The Clean Sweep effort was launched as a cooperative venture. The program began with the dispatching of officers to secure the perimeter and interior areas of a target building. Next, housing officials inspected each unit and public areas, ensuring that only legitimate leaseholders occupied the building. (Police would then make arrests for trespassing at that time if necessary.) Housing officials then secured the building, creating a single entry/exit where a security station was set up to restrict access to residents (who were issued identification cards) and accompanied guests (Lane, 1989). As a result of the cooperative program, crime immediately fell by 32 percent (U.S. HUD, 1989a).

Crafting an organized approach so that each element occurs at an appointed time, and so that each actor has a specific role, is part of the art of implementing responses that produce results.

Evaluate Progress

It is important to recognize that conditions which give rise to problems in these neighborhoods are historical and ongoing. It is unlikely that big problems in dysfunctional communities can be completely solved, nor be fully solved by police; but it is entirely possible that the harm related to these problems can be lessened, and problems can be managed. Within this context, the collaborative goals of police and other agencies should be established as part of an on-going effort, rather than short-term.

Once a response has been implemented, the important question to ask is: What are the results? Results are usually measurable in terms of the goals that were established. For example, if the goal was to control ingress to buildings, was that objective achieved? Do spot checks of leases and residences reveal that outsiders have been successfully excluded from the buildings? Do residents feel safer? Do residents perceive that outsiders are excluded? Are arrests still mostly of non-residents? Was a security system successfully developed and implemented? Is there a full-time guard monitoring ingress?

If one has developed a clearly defined goal, it is much easier to define success (or a lack of success). Measuring and documenting results is extremely important because it provides evidence of the police effort to elected officials and agency heads. It also provides fodder for the continuation of police efforts, suggests modification of plans for further efforts, sparks hope in the affected communities, and may encourage other individuals and groups to get involved in similar problem-solving efforts.

Success can be measured in a variety of ways. The easiest measure is to ask, "Did the crime rate fall?" Whether police look at reported property crime or violent crime, these statistics are convenient measures if crime reduction was the goal that was sought by the response.

A rise and fall in calls for service may be a useful measure of results. Calls for service, however, may rise following police initiatives because residents may feel police are more willing to take action. However, the types of calls for service may vary, so one should evaluate the kind of calls for service along with the frequency.

Just as calls for service may be misleading, a rise or fall in arrests may not be an accurate measure of success. Arrest statistics can reflect a measure of immediate police effort, not police effectiveness.

Success can be measured in less traditional ways. For example, successes can be measured visually. Photographs, for example, are good evidence of improved conditions in poor areas. Surveys of residents are an especially useful measure, because they can document levels of fear that exist in communities. Police may also consider other, less direct indicators of improved conditions in poor neighborhoods. For example, counting the number of children in recreational playgrounds before and after a program is implemented may mirror attitudes of fear. Since residents have the best information about illegal activity in the community, there may be substantial differences in their willingness to allow small children out to play before and after police initiatives.

Other good measures range from a visual assessment of the physical environment to recording the frequency of gunshots, rise or fall in rates of treatment for drug-related problems within the catchment area, incidence of gunshot and other violently inflicted woundings linked with drug dealing, or a fall in accidental deaths (overdoses). In the long term, other measures may indicate successful initiatives, for example, occupancy rates for apartments may increase if drug-related problems are abated.

There are many sources of good measures for evaluation. Skillful problem solvers will give thought to these measures prior to implementation. Two primary techniques used for evaluation are a (1) before-and-after technique and a (2) comparison group.

In a before-and-after evaluation, information is collected about the various elements of the problem which are likely to be affected by the response. For example, if the goal is to reduce the number of drug hot spots in a specific community, perhaps those that are outdoors, one might count the number of hot spots in that community. Information could be collected about those hot spot locations, including typical number of dealers, age of dealers, drug of choice and price, frequency of customers and so forth. After the response is implemented, the hot spots would be counted again. Information about each of the measures would again be collected to determine if the hot spots were eliminated, or reduced or changed in some way, or if they had simply moved to another area.

The second evaluation technique is to use a control or comparison matched group to compare the results of the response in the target area. Thus, for example, if a response were being implemented in one public housing community, another similar community could be selected as a control group. The control community should be as similar as possible in terms of size, demographic and socioeconomic composition, layout and design of the buildings, and other characteristics. Information is then collected about both the target community and the control community on a number of measures such as crime, calls for service, levels of fear, and so forth, again depending upon the objective of the response. After the response is implemented, information is again collected on these same measures for both the target and the control community. These figures should reveal whether the same results occurred in both communities. For example, if violent crime fell in the target community following implementation of a response, but stayed the same in the control community, one can more confidently link the response with the fall in violent crime.

One should also make an effort to document whether the problem in the target community was eliminated, reduced or simply moved to another location. Good evaluation techniques help with this documentation. There is certainly a possibility that a problem tackled by police has only been relocated to another area. If, indeed, displacement occurs (and such displacement should be carefully documented rather than assumed as a natural result), police should recognize that new problems need time to take root. Relocated drug dealers need time before their customers determine their location, and these dealers are much more fragile to police and community intervention when they have just set up shop. Thus, even if displacement occurs, there are still some benefits associated with the original police effort.

Frustrations and Roadblocks

The path to success in implementing police initiatives in public housing is an obstacle course with many hurdles. Police should always remember that the problems in many of these poor neighborhoods have been there for many years and are deeply rooted in poverty and other enduring social problems. There are real limits to what the police can actually accomplish and it is extremely unlikely that any of these larger issues will be solved. Not all problems can be solved; some, however, can be managed or made less troubling to the affected community.

Thus, it is important to set modest objectives and take pride in even very small successes in troubled areas. Because drug problems are particularly complex and enduring problems in poor neighborhoods, modest successes are very important. These small successes are instrumental in improving the quality of life for the people who reside in the drug-ravaged areas. If police try to reduce the harms caused by drug dealing in a specific area, great strides can be made in terms of improving the lives of the law-abiding citizens who call the community home.

VI.

Police Strategies Vary

Faced with the challenges of policing low income housing communities, some police departments have developed creative strategies that cross the boundaries of traditional law enforcement strategies. Most of these responses have been developed with close collaboration between police and housing officials; on some occasions, residents have been involved in the process. Of anti-drug initiatives being conducted by local PHAs (reported to HUD in mid-1989), more than one-third of the reporting agencies said they were actively involved with law enforcement efforts. Police have also reached out to a variety of other organizations to direct resources towards problems located in these specific areas.

Because many police strategies have been tried around the country, the framework of responses developed in Chapter V is useful for reviewing and evaluating potential strategies. It is likely that a police initiative to deal with specific drug-related problems in public housing might include a number of these strategies, reshaped to fit the particular needs of the community and to make use of available resources.

Improving Physical Environment

A number of police agencies have focused on improving the physical environment of public housing. Because certain physical problems are viewed as being linked with drug dealing and give rise to fear within the law-abiding public housing community, police have put these environmental problems high on a list of options.

For example, police officers in Tampa, FL, recognizing that drug dealing was often shrouded by poor exterior lighting, conducted a survey of lighting in a troubled public housing complex. The officers enlisted assistance from the local utility company and the city to have the lighting upgraded in wattage and broken lights repaired. Now, lights are evaluated routinely to ensure adequate lighting in the community.

In some cities, officers routinely identify privately-owned abandoned buildings and inform the city's codes and compliance agency to have the buildings demolished. In public housing agencies, once a unit is abandoned, deterioration sets in quickly. To avoid the residence becoming physically devastated by vandalism, or being used by drug dealers or users, housing agencies often attempt to have the units quickly boarded up. In Tulsa, OK, officers routinely check apartments to ensure that neither vagrants nor dealers have taken over the property.

Officers in Atlanta, GA, and Tampa, FL, concerned that trash-strewn lots provided easy hiding places for drugs, organized a clean up effort in a public housing community (Huguley, 1989; Tampa Police Dept., 1989). Officers in Philadelphia, PA, developed an on-going program directed at removing abandoned cars from public housing areas. The cars were often used as drug caches.

In many cities, including Chicago, police have worked with housing officials to develop access control for buildings. By limiting entrances and exits to one per building, non-residents can be kept outside. This approach is most adaptable to high rise buildings. Some housing agencies, however, have experimented with fencing and other methods to control foot traffic in the public housing community. In a North Charleston, SC, public housing complex, a private developer erected an 8-foot fence of brick, iron and chain link; along with other security measures, the fence is credited with producing a reduction in street dealing. Some agencies have adapted identification cards for their residents so that outsiders can be systematically excluded from the property. Police can help design and implement these programs.

Remove Offenders

Removing drug dealers is often a top goal of both police, the public housing agency, and residents. It is a goal that has been tackled in several different ways.

Increased enforcement/prosecution. The first line of police response to concentrated problems is to beef up enforcement. A number of police agencies respond to drug problems by increasing the number of officers assigned to an area, i.e., by "occupying" the community.

Other law enforcement agencies have increased enforcement through assigning foot patrol officers to public housing areas or establishing mini-stations within the complexes. Frequently, the housing authority will make an apartment available for a mini-station or for police use so that a more visible police presence can be established within the community. The Orlando (FL) Police Department has substations in vacant units of three different housing complexes; the police logo is painted on these exterior of the unit and a police cruiser is parked nearby. Similar units have been used in Newport News, VA, New Brunswick, NJ, Alexandria, VA, and Monette, AR.

Some law enforcement agencies, in concert with the housing agency or residents, have designated targeted drug free zones (DFZs) where enforcement and community efforts are focused. Modeled after the idea of drug-free areas around schools, where arrests for drug dealing carry increased penalties and patrol efforts are concentrated, these zones can provide an oasis for residents in the community. The Philadelphia Police Department has used this strategy in South Philadelphia; the housing authority of New Orleans has designated DFZs and targeted the most dangerous and drug-infested areas. The city of Baltimore is also experimenting with this strategy.

Another strategy that targets a small geographic area is known as "Oasis." The Oasis program has been used in Fort Lauderdale, Tampa, and Louisville, KY. It is an approach that includes analyzing slum areas, building a coalition with community groups and police, and developing drug-free oases as an initial step toward a safer community. The oases are intended to have a domino effect over time until the larger community becomes revitalized.

A number of police agencies have beefed up enforcement by using undercover officers and buy-bust techniques to make arrests of dealers in public housing. Other police agencies have focused on improving their ability to enforce trespass laws in public housing. As a designated agent of the housing authority, police agencies in cities such as Tampa, Atlanta, and Baltimore, can focus on trespassing enforcement, and secure cooperation from the judiciary to impose stiff penalties for trespassing. Other agencies have other laws in their cities, for example, youth curfews or loitering ordinances, which they can rigidly enforce to deal with specific problems.

Beefing up enforcement efforts often goes hand in hand with securing penalties from the judiciary. A number of police agencies, such as Orleans Parish, LA, developed collaborative relations with the judiciary to ensure that first time offenders were punished. Other agencies have gotten the judiciary to impose minimum sentences for drug dealing.

Asset seizures. Seizing the assets of drug dealers in low income communities is one strategy which local law enforcement agencies are increasingly using to tackle drug problems. Law enforcement agencies use state forfeiture laws, or federal laws which allow them to share seized property with the Justice Department and Customs Service. Asset forfeiture is perceived as being an effective way, not only to punish the drug dealers, but to set an example to youth in the community. Seizing the assets of dealers who may be viewed as role models of success in a poor community sends a strong message to the community.

Assets seized range from boats, cars, planes, and land to cash. The funds derived from seized assets enable many local law enforcement agencies to increase narcotics funds or fund capital expenditures.

Lease Enforcement. Lease enforcement is one of the primary ways in which police and housing officials have attempted to oust drug dealing tenants from public housing.

In Atlanta, the police department has a detective who is assigned full-time to the housing authority and who serves as a staff liaison between the two agencies. The detective has office space in the PHA offices and works closely with the PHA's director of security, ensuring communication about arrests of tenants. Although the department's computer capability is limited, the PHA-police team reviews all arrest data to expedite the eviction process (Huguley, 1989). In San Francisco, housing authority staff provide city police with a list of vacant units to assist in arresting drug dealers who may be using the apartments (U.S. HUD, 1989a).

Police information can also be useful to housing agencies in the process of screening residents, and in hiring housing staff.

Some housing authorities have specifically strengthened their leases, to expressly prohibit residents from engaging in drug-related activity. This lease provision gives housing and police more power to evict criminals from public housing. In April 1989, HUD established a notice that leases must include an explicit provision allowing eviction if any member of the household or person under the tenant's control engages in drug-related criminal activity.

An issue in evicting drug dealers from public housing is the problem of evicting a family in which only one family member may be engaging in drug activity. One typical case was reported, for example, where a grandmother was evicted because her grandson was involved in drug dealing. Housing officials reply that in such a case, the grandmother should have the youth's name removed from the lease to avoid being evicted for a lease violation. The reverse side of the coin, however, is that some families may become homeless if ousted for one member's illegal behavior. This issue is a thorny one between PHA and some residents, and police should tread lightly on the topic.

Some housing agencies, concerned that evicted families would go apartment hopping, have established data banks to track tenants in public and subsidized housing. The Northern California and Nevada Public Housing Directors Association and Association of Housing Management Agents, for example, contracted to have such a data bank maintained so that agencies could check the status of applicants who apply for public or subsidized housing.

Another method for keeping trespassers out of public housing has been to develop and implement car registration programs. Among others, this program has been conducted in Denison, TX, Greensboro, GA, Clearwater and Tampa, FL.

Making it Inconvenient. Other methods of deterring drug dealers from specific neighborhoods may be as simple as determining what dealers do business in a certain location. For example, San Diego police discovered that drug dealers were clustered around the public telephones on certain street corners. Upon learning that the dealers used the phones to receive orders, the San Diego police pursued an initiative to have the phones dedicated to only outgoing calls, preventing drug dealers from receiving orders by phone. It was a simple tactic that improved the neighborhood and gave citizens access to the telephones once more.

Reduce Demand

Reducing the demand for drugs in public housing means focusing efforts on those individuals who do not sell the drugs, but those who use the drugs or who may become drug users.

Sting Operations. A number of police agencies have begun to make use of undercover officers to conduct reverse buy-busts, or sting operations. In this strategy, drug buyers who purchase illegal drugs in these neighborhoods are arrested. Miami, FL, and Birmingham, AL, are two law enforcement agencies which have popularized the reverse buy operation. Some agencies also use forfeiture laws to seize assets of drug buyers.

Ethical and legal questions do arise with reverse buys. For example, law enforcement agencies must determine whether to "sell" an inert look-alike drug, or the real drug, and consider what liability exposure the agency will encounter.

Educating Users. A number of demand reduction strategies are aimed at educating users and potential users about the dangers of using drugs. Many people point to the success of the DARE (Drug Abuse Resistance Education) program in Los Angeles. DARE has spread to many other cities around the country. In the DARE programs, uniformed law enforcement officers go into the schools to work with youths to deter drug use. "Just Say No" groups and other drug education groups are popular and police at all levels are engaged in this type of programming.

Youth Diversion. Other demand reduction strategies are basically youth diversion programs. This category of response focuses on providing some alternative activities for youth. These options are intended to replace drug-related activity. These diversions may take the shape of recreational activity or equipment, school programs, scouting activities and similar programs. Police have often been instrumental in determining the need for and tapping the resources to launch these types of programs.

Some police agencies have linked youthful drug dealing activities with drop out and truancy problems in area schools. Through contacting the schools to develop a collaborative initiative, these problems have been somewhat mitigated.

Treatment. Treatment and rehabilitation is a final category of a demand reduction strategy. In some police agencies, officers refer drug users to clinics, hospitals, treatment programs or other groups such as Narcotics Anonymous. In many communities, knowledge among residents of these facilities may be quite limited. (Indeed, often resources are quite limited.)

Improve Intelligence

In Nashville, TN, police developed and held training sessions for residents of public housing complexes. The goal of the training was to teach tenants about the police. Addressed were issues of obtaining search warrants, standard operating procedures for responding to certain classes of calls, the concept of probable cause, and the necessity of evidence. Police took time to explain to residents why drug dealers were often arrested and back on the streets within hours — a circumstance that had led residents to believe police were in cahoots with the drug dealers. The goal was to improve the communication of information between citizens and police and to further the notion that police are on the same side with the citizens.

Community Surveys. Many police departments, including the San Diego and Tulsa police departments, have conducted residential surveys in low income neighborhoods to obtain more information about problems from the residents.

In the Newport News burglary problem discussed earlier, police officers conducted a community survey of a large low income apartment complex. One important result of the survey was that officers developed empathy for some of the residents when they discovered there were in fact some "good guys" living in these units. The officers also were able to see for themselves the physical deterioration in which tenants were forced to live by observing the physical elements that were beyond the control of the individual such as faulty window structure and dilapidated flooring.

In conducting a community survey in a public housing complex in Tampa, officers were able to spend time with residents one-on-one, developing a personal rapport that was anticipated to lead to a police-community support system within a neighborhood that had been antagonistic to police efforts.

Tip Lines. In some communities, police have established special telephone lines to take information from residents to protect their anonymity. This practice avoids any potential for criminals in the complexes to learn who has reported information to the police. If used, these numbers should be circulated widely among residents.

In Dorchester, MA, low income residents make use of a tip line, called Drop-A-Dime, which funnels information about drug dealing to local police. Police make a formal report to the Drop-A-Dime organization

Pride of Ownership May Reduce Crime

The concept of management and ownership of public housing units by public housing residents is a notion being advanced by Jack Kemp, secretary of the U.S. Department of Housing and Urban Development.

Although experimentation with the management/ ownership concept has been limited, several applications of the idea show promise. For example, in Washington, D.C., residents formed a management group and began operating the Kenilworth-Parkside public housing complex. Under their management, between 1982 and 1985, rental collections increased 77 percent, vacancy rates dropped 70 percent and welfare dependency dropped from 85 percent to 5 percent (Woodson, 1988). Crime in the complex has also fallen dramatically. In fact, Kenilworth-Parkside residents are credited with having "run most dope dealers away" (Davidson, 1989a; Woodson, 1988).

The underlying foundation for tenant management and ownership is that residents have a stake in the each month about the disposition of the calls. A number of arrests are credited to the tip effort.

In Kansas City, MO, a group known as the Ad Hoc Group Against Crime formed a close alliance with police. The group has a 24-hour "Secret Witness" telephone hotline for people who have information about crime. An arrest and conviction can lead to a reward; another program offers support to victims and witnesses of violent crimes, and can recommend, if necessary, the use of funds to relocate these individuals. These programs have produced good information for police.

well-being of the property once they are owners and managers. "It's more pride if you own something yourself," said a Kenilworth-Parkside resident (Davidson, 1989a).

Kemp has been a strong supporter of resident management and ownership. Critics claim that successes in resident management and ownership initiatives are linked only with individual charismatic leadership. For example, in Washington, that leadership has taken the form of Kimi Gray; in St. Louis, Bertha Gilkey is credited with the success of resident management. Other critics caution that resident ownership will only serve to further reduce the nation's dwindling stock of public housing units, to the disadvantage of poor renters.

Whether resident management/ownership initiatives can in fact transcend the charismatic leadership of a few, and whether funds to support these initiatives will continue to be dedicated, remains to be seen. But it may be a good approach with benefits for the entire community.

Improve Reporting. In Philadelphia, police developed a radio bypass of police communication so that beat officers could be telephoned directly by citizens for calls that would have been assigned a low priority by police dispatch.

Police can also improve the information they receive about problems in other ways. Intelligence can be increased by unusual procedures. Police have been known to interview arrestees to obtain inside information on how certain criminal activities are conducted. In other agencies, arrestees have been interviewed in jail with a jail debriefing form. This kind of data is useful as police continue to document the link between drugs and criminal activity.

Housing personnel are often the closest to drug problems in public housing. These housing personnel can be trained to identify drugs or drug dealing behaviors, and cooperate with police in following up on complaints.

Intelligence information can also be improved by facilitating the communication between narcotics investigators and patrol officers. For example, in Atlanta, a narcotics supervisor recognized that patrol and narcotics had historically used a different radio frequency and were unable to communicate. The problem was quickly corrected.

Empower Residents

Police agencies in a number of cities around the country have become engaged in activities of identifying and directing resources designed to empower residents to regain control of their neighborhoods. This category of response is subject to the criticism of having police officers engage in social work; however, targeting the broader needs of poor residents is considered an important priority within some police agencies.

In point of fact, this type of police response can serve several different purposes. This response can bring the police into closer contact with the residents, and contribute to enhanced feelings of trust; police can sometimes gain access to resources from which residents may feel excluded or lack information about; and, these responses may get at some of the underlying conditions which give rise to drug-related problems.

For example, in Philadelphia, police believe that youths in poor communities need positive role models. Police developed a relationship with a group called Concerned Black Men to bring black male role models into the community.

In Tulsa, one officer identified a problem of low self-esteem among the teenage females in public housing. As a response to that problem, the officer started a program known as the Young Ladies Self Awareness Organization. Other officers in Tulsa decided that limited job opportunities were a problem in the city's public housing because youths were unable to find jobs. The officers now steer youths into Job Corps, a training and job program, and alternative schooling environments.

Application

This list of police initiatives in public housing is incomplete and infinitely expandable. None of the strategies described are intended to be prescriptive responses for dealing with drug-related problems in public housing. Some of these strategies are effective in some communities because they meet very specific objectives. It is possible that a combination of several of these strategies, tailored and fine-tuned to the community in which they are applied, may yield some positive results in terms of affecting problems linked with drug dealing. However, each initiative should be carefully assessed to determine how well it may work in the targeted community, how effectively it makes use of existing resources, and to determine that measurable results are being achieved.

Appendix A

Subsidized Housing Exceeds Public Housing

Public housing is the most familiar type of public assistance for housing visible to middle-class America. It is certainly a vivid symbol of the government's provision of housing for the poor; yet, newer subsidized housing programs provide more housing for poor families in America than does conventional public housing. Most often, these subsidized units are privately-owned although publicly subsidized; they are more frequently located in scattered sites rather than densely sited. These other types of housing programs for the poor sometimes generate just as many problems, including crime problems, as do public housing. But there are some key differences between the programs.

The traditional public housing is known as "conventional public housing" or the "Low Rent Public Housing program"; privately-owned housing occupied by federally-subsidized tenants is known as "publicly-assisted housing" or "assisted housing." Assisted housing programs include the Section 8 Existing Housing Certificate Program and the Housing Voucher Program. The key difference is that in public housing, the PHA is the landlord; in these two Section 8 programs, the voucher program and the existing certificate, the private owner is the landlord for the property.

These two Section 8 programs subsidized nearly 1 million American households in 1987 as compared to 1.4 million units of public housing. The largest of these programs, the Section 8 Existing Certificate, served about 800,000 families. The voucher program is much newer; slightly more than 100,000 families receive vouchers (U.S. HUD, 1989d: 39-41).

KEY STEPS FOR OBTAINING SUBSIDIZED HOUSING

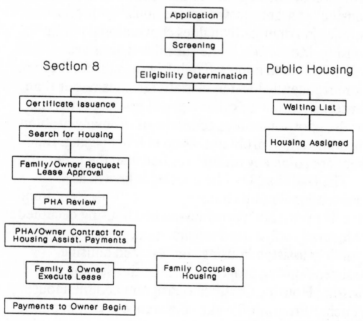

Adapted From Quadel Consulting,
Coursebook for Rent Specialists

114

Subsidized housing basically got its start in the mid-1960s. Because of the rising operating costs associated with operating public housing, beginning in 1965, a leased housing component was added to the programs administered by the PHAs. The program was intended to limit the number of units to be leased in a single privately-owned facility in an effort to disperse public housing tenants. Thus scattered dwellings would reduce the isolation and alienation often felt by public housing tenants and serve to integrate these subsidized tenants into the larger community.

To participate in the public housing program, a needy family applies to the local PHA. The PHA reviews the application, and determines eligibility, primarily on the basis of income and family size. If approved, the family is provided an apartment and must pay 30 percent of their adjusted income for rent, including utilities.

For its primary subsidized housing program, Section 8 Existing Certificate, participants apply and their eligibility is determined. Eligibility for the program is limited to families who earn less than 50 percent of the median income in the area where housing is sought (National Association of Housing and Redevelopment Officials, 1988: 15).

If the family is approved for subsidized housing through Section 8, they are eventually issued a "certificate of participation" and are free to rent whatever unit desired, up to a ceiling rent (U.S. HUD, 1982). The family then looks for an apartment, and submits a lease to be reviewed by the PHA. The review ensures that a fair market rent is being charged and that the dwelling meets federal requirements of safety and sanitation.

Under this program, HUD pays the difference between what the family can afford (that is, 30 percent of their income) and the rent for the apartment. Rents for the unit (including utilities) must be at or below a fair market rent determined by HUD for the area and must also be comparable to rents paid for comparable units.

The Section 8 Housing Voucher program is similar to Section 8 Existing Certificate. However, the voucher program provides families with a greater choice in selecting their apartment. Families can choose units with rents above the fair market rent and pay the difference, or can rent a cheaper apartment and pay less than 30 percent of their income. Again, HUD's payments for this program are based on the difference between the standard rent for the area and 30 percent of the family's adjusted income.

For each of these housing programs for the poor (as with public housing), preference is given to some families, such as those who occupy substandard housing, are involuntarily displaced, or pay more than half their income for rent. Some PHAs must also give preference to the homeless. Each year, the PHA reviews the subsidized family to reevaluate its financial condition. For the subsidized housing programs, the PHA's role is basically limited to determining tenant eligibility and issuing certificates. Their function is also to conduct initial property inspections and process payments to landlords.

HUD's Section 8 Existing Certificate program is the department's major vehicle for the delivery of rental subsidies to low income families. The program has grown rapidly since its inception in 1974; it now serves almost as many families as conventional public housing.

The demand for housing vouchers is also high. For fiscal year 1989, the Administration had proposed 100,000 additional subsidy vouchers; estimates, however, were that New York City alone could use more than 500,000, according to Irving Welfeld. (However, a recent study of recipients of housing certificates and vouchers revealed that as many as 40 percent ofvoucher recipients were unable to use them because they simply could not locate housing that met the federal standards of quality within the fair market rent limitations (Welfeld, 1988: 92).)

None of the housing assistance programs has kept pace with the demand for low cost housing. In fact, although more than 4 million households in the country participate in some type of federally subsidized housing program, this figure represents only 20 percent of those households which are eligible (U.S. HUD, 1989b).

Appendix B

Who's Responsible?

Determining just which agency provides what services to public housing residents is sometimes a source of conflict between city agencies and PHAs. For example, the Housing Act of 1937 specifies that a PHA's operations include "any or all undertakings appropriate for management, operation, services, maintenance, security (including the cost of security personnel) or financing in connection with a lower income housing project...To the maximum extent available and appropriate, public and private agencies in the community should be used for the provision of such services" [U.S. Housing Act of 1937, Sec. 3, (8)(c) (2)]. It is easy to see how confusion might arise over interpretation of the Act. However, by statute, a formal cooperative agreement between city and PHA is required. This document spells out the relationship between city and housing agency (Meehan, 1985: 291).

The International City Management Association defines nine major functional areas for PHAs. One of these is security: "Security encompasses attempts to reduce crime, antisocial behavior, and vandalism within the housing sites. The main objectives are protection of people and property, and services are generally delivered by a separate cadre of personnel and by special physical arrangement of installations. Specific activities include surveillance and/or personal inspection of all the properties on a regular schedule; handling requests for assistance; coordination and cooperation with local police departments; and work with tenants and community organizations to increase awareness of responsibilities and potential for improved security (Arnold, 1982: 222).

Glossary of terms

Authority — A Public Housing Authority is the agency which operates public housing in a specific area.

Certificate — This term refers to the assistance provided by the Section 8 Certificate program which encourages eligible very low-income families to negotiate directly with private landlords to secure rental housing.

CIAP — The Comprehensive Improvement Assistance Program, known as CIAP, is the federal aid provided to PHAs to finance capital improvements in public housing projects.

Defensible Space — This is an area which, because of real or symbolic barriers, is considered to be under the control and surveillance of residents.

Density — The number of units per building, per block, or per square mile. Density is an indicator of how closely people have to live together.

Eviction — An eviction is the formal process for having a tenant removed from a public housing unit. Just as with an eviction from a privately-owned dwelling, an eviction is a legal process.

Grievance — The formal process to which a tenant is entitled when being evicted from public housing. In some PHAs, there is a formal grievance procedure; however, in most states, residents are fully protected by a state's due process laws. HUD can waive a PHA's grievance procedure if it is determined that tenants are adequately protected by state laws.

Head of Household — This term refers to the person who holds the lease for a unit in public housing. Head of household contrasts with the term resident, which refers to all the occupants (named on the lease) of a public housing unit, such as children of the household head.

HUD — The term HUD refers to the U.S. Department of Housing and Urban Development in Washington, DC, or one of the agency's ten regional offices.

Lower Income — HUD sets at 80 percent of the median income for the area. Families with Lower Income may be granted exceptions by HUD and participate in the Section 8 program.

Operating Funds — The money needed for the day-to-day operations of public housing, such as maintenance, administrative costs, and so forth.

PHA — Public Housing Authority is the agency which operates public housing in a community.

PILOT — Payment in Lieu of Taxes. PHAs have PILOT contracts with local governments to make a payment in lieu of taxes equal to 10 percent of gross rent less utilities.

Poor — A family or individual living at or below the poverty line of $11,201 for a family of four, $5,572 for an individual.

Resident — Refers to all the individuals who legally live in public housing. The term does not include those who illegally live in the complexes.

Resident management — This term refers to public housing which is operated to a varying extent by the residents of the public housing complex.

Section 8 — This is a housing program known as Lower-Income Rental Assistance that helps low and very low income families obtain privately-owned housing. The two major forms of this program are Section 8 housing vouchers and Section 8 housing certificates.

Subsidy — In the Section 8 program, the portion the PHA pays of the family's rent which is the difference between the rent the owner charges and the family's share of the rent. Local PHAs also receive annual subsidies from HUD.

Very Low Income — HUD's term for a family income (adjusted for size) of 50 percent or less of the median income for the area. Very low income at admission to Section 8 programs is determined by family size for the area in which the PHA is located.

Voucher — This term refers to the Section 8 Housing voucher program which assists very low income families in renting privately-owned housing.

SELECTED BIBLIOGRAPHY

Allen, K. (1989) **The Scope and Effect of Tulsa, Oklahoma's Drug Problem: Drug Problem Inventory,** Tulsa, OK: Tulsa Police Department.

Arnold, D.S., Ed., (1982) **Housing and Local Government,** Washington, D.C.: International City Management Association.

Atlanta Housing Authority. (nd) **Quality Service is Our Bottom Line,** Atlanta, GA: author.

Bain, D., Battaglia, M., Merrill, S., Scardino, V. & Wallace, J. (1988) **Study of the Modernization Needs of the Public and Indian Housing Stock,** Washington, D.C.: U.S. Department of Housing and Urban Development, Office of Policy Development and Research, HUD-1130-PDR, March.

Baxter, T. (1989) How Crack has Recast Black Politics. **The Atlanta Journal & Constitution,** April 30.

Berke, R. (1989) Housing Agency to Widen Drive On Drugs Into Private Operations. **The New York Times,** May 31.

Boston Housing Authority. (1988) **Meeting the Promise: BHA 1987 Annual Report,** Boston, MA: Author.

Bratt, R. (1986) Public Housing: The Controversy and Contribution. In R. Bratt, C. Hartman, A. Mayerson (Eds.), **Critical Perspectives on Housing,** Philadelphia: Temple University Press, 335-361.

Brill, W. (1973) Security in Public Housing: A
Synergistic Approach. **Deterrence of Crime In and
Around Residences,** Washington D.C.: U.S.
Department of Justice, Law Enforcement
Assistance Administration (June), 26-44.

Brill Associates, Inc., William. (1977) **Victimization,
Fear of Crime and Altered Behavior: A Profile of
the Crime Problem in William Nickerson Jr.
Gardens, Los Angeles, CA,** Washington, D.C.: U.S.
Department of Housing and Urban Development,
Office of Policy Development, September.

Brown, N. (1989) **Testimony at Public Hearing on the
Drug Problem and Public Housing.** U.S. House of
Representatives Select Committee On Narcotics
Abuse and Control, Washington D.C., June 15.

Burton, C. (1988) Up and at 'Em: Housing Cops Exit
Lobbies to Fight Crime. **Philadelphia Daily News**
(June 10), 8.

Caprara, D. & Alexander B. (1989) **Empowering
Residents of Public Housing: A Resource Guide for
Resident Management,** Washington, D.C.: National
Center for Neighborhood Enterprise.

Clark, J. (1989) Springtime Means Housecleaning. **Law
Enforcement News**
(May 15), 1.

Currie, E. (1989) Confronting Crime: Looking Toward
the Twenty-First Century. **Justice Quarterly,**
Volume 6, No. 1, March.

Davidson, J. (1989a) Takeover by Tenants of Housing Project Makes Place Livable. **The Wall Street Journal**, (July 6), A1.

Davidson, J. (1989b) Public Housing Aides Push to Evict Drug Users, Sometimes Violating the Rights of Other Tenants. **The Wall Street Journal** (July 6), A14.

Downs, A. (1988) The Housing Challenge. **The Brookings Review**, Washington, D.C.: The Brookings Institution, Winter.

Duggan, D. (1988) Closing Doors on Pushers. **Newsday** (May 1), 3.

Eck, J. & Spelman, W. (1987) **Problem-Solving: Problem-Oriented Policing in Newport News**, Washington D.C.: Police Executive Research Forum.

Fischer, P. (1988) Quality of Life in Housing Has Improved. **The Christian Science Monitor**, Nov. 1.

Garland, S., Therrien, L. & Hammonds, K. (1988) Why the Underclass Can't Get Out From Under. **Businessweek** (Sept. 19), 122-124.

Goldstein, H. (in press) **Problem-Oriented Policing**, forthcoming from New York: McGraw Hill.

Greenberg, S., Rohe, W., & Williams, J. (1982) **Safe and Secure Neighborhoods: Physical Characteristics and Informal Territorial Control in High and Low Crime Neighborhoods,**

Washington D.C.: U.S. Department of Justice, National Institute of Justice, May.

Greenberg, S., Rohe, W., & Williams, J. (1983) Neighborhood Conditions and Community Crime Control. **Community Crime Prevention,** Washington D.C.: CRG Press, 5-8.

Greenberg, S., Rohe, W., & Williams, J. (1985) **Informal Citizen Action and Crime Prevention at the Neighborhood Level: Synthesis and Assessment of the Research,** Washington D.C.: U.S. Department of Justice, National Institute of Justice, March.

Higdon, R. & Huber, P. (1987) **How to Fight Fear: The Citizen Oriented Police Enforcement Program Package,** Washington D.C.: Police Executive Research Forum, May.

Hoffman, D. (1988) Gangs, Drugs Rule Comanche Park, Tenants Tell Randle. **Tulsa World** (Nov. 4), D1.

Hughes, M., (1989) **Poverty in Cities,** Washington D.C.: National League of Cities.

Huguley, S. (1989) **Illegal Drugs In Atlanta,** Atlanta, GA: Atlanta Bureau of Police Services.

Institute for Law and Justice, Inc. (1988) **NIJ Quick Response Assessment of the Oasis Project in Louisville, Kentucky,** Alexandria, VA: U.S. Department of Justice, National Institute of Justice, March.

Jackson, A. (1988) Kenilworth-Parkside: Success Story or Cruel Charade? **The Washington Post**, Nov. 3.

Jaynes, G. and Williams, R. (1989) **A Common Destiny: Blacks and American Society**. Washington, D.C.: National Academy Press.

Kaplan, J. (1988) Taking Drugs Seriously. **The Public Interest** (Summer), 32-51.

Kleiman, M. & Putala, C. (1987) **State and Local Drug Law Enforcement: Issues and Practices**, Working Paper #87-01-06, March.

Kolodny, R., Baron, R. & Struyk, R. (1983a) **The Insider's Guide To Managing Public Housing - Volume One**, Washington, D.C.: U.S. Department of Housing and Urban Development, Office of Policy Development and Research, HUD-PDR-638, August.

Kolodny, R., Baron, R. & Struyk, R. (1983b) **The Insider's Guide To Managing Public Housing - Volume Two**, Washington, D.C.: U.S. Department of Housing and Urban Development, Office of Policy Development and Research, HUD-PDR-639, August.

Kotlowitz, A. (1988) Lords of the Slum: Chicago Street Gangs Treat Public Housing As Private Fortresses. **The Wall Street Journal**, Sept. 30.

Kuhn, A. (1988) PHA Management: Are the Critics Right? **Journal of Housing** (March/April), 67-74.

Kurtz, H. (1988) Learning to Live With Less: Budget Cuts Have Limited Impact In Newark. **The Washington Post,** June 1.

Lane, V. (1989) **Testimony at Public Hearing on the Drug Problem and Public Housing.** U.S. House of Representatives Select Committee On Narcotics Abuse and Control, Washington D.C., June 15.

Lemann, N. (1986) The Origins of the Underclass. **The Atlantic Monthly,** (June), 31-68.

Lemann, N. (1988) The Unfinished War, Part I. **The Atlantic Monthly** (December), 37-56.

Lemann, N. (1989) The Unfinished War, Part II. **The Atlantic Monthly** (January), 53-68.

Locked Out, Locked Up. (1988) **New York Daily News,** April 30.

Loux, S. & Sadacca, R. (1979) **Comparison of Public Housing Tenant Characteristics: 1976 To 1979,** Washington D.C.: The Urban Institute, August.

Meehan, E. (1985) The Evolution of Public Housing Policy. In P. Mitchell (Ed.), **Federal Housing Policy and Programs, Past and Present,** New Jersey: Rutgers University Press, 287-318.

Meeks, J. and Hasson, M. (1989) **Drug Problem Inventory Report,** Philadelphia, PA: Philadelphia Police Department.

Misner, G. (1973) Community Involvement in Crime Prevention. **Deterrence of Crime In and Around Residences**, Washington D.C.: U.S. Department of Justice, Law Enforcement Assistance Administration (June), 44-52.

Moore, M. (1988) Drug Trafficking. **Crime File Study Guide**, Washington, D.C.: U.S. Department of Justice/National Institute of Justice.

Moore, M. (1988) The Police and Drugs: In Search Of A Strategy, A Working Paper For Discussion, Nov. 21.

Moore, M. & Trojanowicz, R. (1988) Policing and the Fear of Crime. **Perspectives on Policing**, Washington D.C.: U.S. Department of Justice, National Institute of Justice, Washington D.C., June.

Nadelmann, E. (1988) The Case for Legalization. **The Public Interest**, (Summer), 3-32.

National Association of Housing and Redevelopment Officials. (1988) Keeping the Commitment: An Action Plan for Better Housing and Communities for All. **Journal of Housing**, January/February.

National Criminal Justice Association. (1988) Confined Youth. **Justice Bulletin** (November), 3-8.

National Housing Task Force. (1988) **A Decent Place to Live: The Report of the National Housing Task Force**, Washington D.C.: Author, March.

Newman, O. (1973) **Defensible Space: Crime Prevention Through Urban Design**. New York: Collier Books.

Peattie, L. (1972) **Conventional Public Housing**, Joint Center Working Paper No. 3 for the Subcommittee on Housing of the Committee on Banking and Currency, U.S. House of Representatives, 92nd Congress, February.

Pereira, J. (1988) Boston, Under Pressure, Is Integrating Public Housing. **The Wall Street Journal** (July 12), 36.

Philadelphia Housing Authority. (1988) **Anti-Drug Action Plan for the Philadelphia Housing Authority**, Philadelphia, PA: Author.

Popolizio, E. (1988) At Long Last, A Victory Over the Drug Dealers. **The New York Times**, May 21.

Popolizio, E. (1989) **Testimony at Public Hearing on The Drug Problem and Public Housing**. U.S. House of Representatives Select Committee on Narcotics Abuse and Control, Washington D.C., June 15.

The President's Commission on Housing. (1982) **Report to the President and the Secretary of Housing and Urban Development**, Washington D.C.: Author.

Quadel Consulting Corporation. (n.d.) **Section 8 Existing Housing Program Coursebook For Rent Specialists**, Washington D.C.: U.S. Department of Housing and Urban Development, Existing Housing Division.

Raspberry, W. (1988) The Kenilworth Story. **The Washington Post**, Oct. 31.

Robinson, M. (1986) **Case Studies of Effective Management Practices within Public Housing Agencies - Volume Six:** Security, Washington, D.C.: U.S. Department of Housing and Urban Development, Office of Policy Development and Research, HUD-1053-PDR(2), November.

Robinson, M. & Toulmin, L. (1986) **Case Studies of Effective Management Practices within Public Housing Agencies - Volume Three:** Rental And Occupancy, Washington, D.C.: U.S. Department of Housing and Urban Development, Office of Policy Development and Research, HUD-1050-PDR(2), November.

Riley, R. (1989) Md. Eviction Policy Prompts Furor. **The Washington Post**, Dec. 18.

Riner, D. (1989) Judge Agrees Mother Had Right to Flee Crime-Filled Project. **The Atlanta Journal & Constitution**, Feb. 18.

Robbins, W. (1989) Goal of a Housing Chief: An Exit to a Better Life. **The New York Times**, Jan. 17.

Russ, V. & Sills, J. (1988) PHA Tenants Tell of Living With Pushers. **Philadelphia Daily News** (June 11), 5.

San Diego Police Department. (1989) **Problem-Oriented Approach To Law Enforcement: Drug Inventory**, San Diego, CA: Author.

Schmidt, W. (1988) Chicago's Housing Raids Challenged. **The New York Times**, Dec. 17.

Shapiro, J. (1989) A Conservative War on Poverty. **U.S. News & World Report** (Feb. 27), 20-23.

Skolnick, J. & Bayley, D. (1988) **Community Policing: Issues and Practices Around the World**, Washington D.C.: U.S. Department of Justice, National Institute of Justice, May.

State College Borough Authority v. Pennsylvania Public Utility Commission. 31.A.2d 557, 562, 152, Pa.Super.363 (1943).

Struyk, R. & Blake, J. (1982) **Determining Who Lives In Public Housing**, Washington D.C.: The Urban Institute.

Taft, P. (1986) **Fighting Fear: The Baltimore County COPE Project**, Washington D.C.: Police Executive Research Forum, February.

Tampa Police Department. (1989) **The Problem-Oriented Approach To Drug Enforcement: Drug Problem Inventory**, Tampa, FL: Author.

Taylor, R. (1982) Neighborhood Physical Environment and Stress. In G. Evans (Ed.), **Environmental Stress**, New York: Cambridge University Press, pp. 286-324.

Tulsa Police Department.(n.d.) **A Guide for Resident Associations, Citizen Oriented Policing Seminars**, Tulsa, OK: Author.

U.S. Department of Housing and Urban Development. (1980) **Social and Economic Characteristics of Residents of Public Housing**, Washington, D.C.: Office of Policy Development and Research, HUD-PDR-537-8, April.

U.S. Department of Housing and Urban Development. (1982) **Evaluation of Leasing Practices in the Section 8 Existing Program**, Washington, D.C.: Office of Policy Development and Research, HUD-PDR-705, September.

U.S. Department of Housing and Urban Development. (1985a) **Comprehensive Improvement Assistance Program: Tenant Training Guidebook**, Washing ton, D.C.: Office of Policy Development and Research, HUD-977-PDR, July.

U.S. Department of Housing and Urban Development. (1985b) **Final Report of the Evaluation of the Urban Initiatives Anti-Crime Demonstration**, Washington, D.C.: Office of Policy Development and Research, HUD-PDR-969, May.

U.S. Department of Housing and Urban Development. (1987) **Lease and Grievance Procedures.** 24 CFR Ch.9. Sec. 966, Washington, D.C.: Office of the Assistant Secretary, April 1.

U.S. Department of Housing and Urban Development. (1988a) **Finding Federally-Assisted Housing,** (Pamphlet) HUD-1149-PIH, Washington D.C.: author, June.

U.S. Department of Housing and Urban Development. (1988b) **HUD Perspective on Public Housing Modernization,** HUD-1142-PDR, Washington, D.C.: Author, March.

U.S. Department of Housing and Urban Development. (1988c) Internal Memorandum: Anti-Drug Abuse Act of 1988, HR 5210. (From Timothy Coyle, Assistant Secretary for Legislation and Congressional Relations), Washington, D.C., Nov. 3.

U.S. Department of Housing and Urban Development. (1988d) Internal Memorandum: Draft List of Responses from Attendees of Regional Drug-Free Public Housing Conferences. Washington, D.C.: Office of General Counsel (Hetty Dick), April 26, 1988.

U.S. Department of Housing and Urban Development. (1989a) Internal Memorandum: Drug Abuse Elimination Efforts: The Public Housing Authorities Respond to Secretary Kemp's Memo. Washington, D.C.: April 17.

U.S. Department of Housing and Urban Development. (1989b) 1987 **National American Housing Survey,** (BOAT Package) Office of Economic Affairs, Office of Paul Burke, May 9.

U.S. Department of Housing and Urban Development. (1989c) **Processing of Applications for Fiscal Year 1989 Funds for Public Housing Resident Management,** Washington, D.C.: Office of Public and Indian Housing, Notice PIH 89-7, Feb. 16.

U.S. Department of Housing and Urban Development. (1989d) **Programs of HUD** 1988-89, HUD-214-PA(16), Washington, D.C.: Author.

U.S. Department of Housing and Urban Development. (1989e) Profile of HUD: **An Introduction to the Major Programs, Organization, Staffing, and Management Systems of the Department of Housing and Urban Development,** Washington, D.C.: Office of Administration, April.

U.S. Department of Housing and Urban Development. (n.d.) **General Information for Commissioners of Low-Income Public Housing Authorities,** Atlanta, GA: Atlanta Regional HUD Office.

U.S. Justice Department. (1989) **Drug Trafficking: A Report to the President of the United States,** Washington, D.C.: Author, August 3.

Venture For Quality Public Housing. (1988) **Security in Public Housing Conference Summary of Baltimore, MD,** Boston, MA: Real Estate Enterprises, Inc., June.

Walker, T. (1989) Times Are Hard for Many in a City of Plenty. **Atlanta Journal & Constitution,** Feb. 13.

Welfeld, I. (1988) Poor Tenants, Poor Landlords, Poor Policy. **The Public Interest** (Summer), 110-121.

Wells, S. (1988a) Drug Trade Out of Control in Low-Income Areas. **The Atlanta Journal & Constitution,** March 27.

Wells, S. (1988b) Housing Authority Meets Federal
    Deadline. **The Atlanta Journal & Constitution,**
    June 29.

Wilson, J. & DiIulio, J. (1989) Crackdown. **The New
    Republic** (July 10), 21-25.

Wilson, W.J. (1987) **The Truly Disadvantaged,**
    Chicago, IL: University of Chicago Press.

Witt, S. (1988) No One Should Live This Way.
    The Tulsa Tribune, Nov. 11.

Woodson, R. (1988) The Kenilworth 'Counterevent.'
    The Washington Post, Nov. 12.

Yen, M. (1988) Housing: More Than A Racial Issue in
    Yonkers. **The Washington Post** (Aug. 22), A1.

DWELLING LEASE

Address of Dwelling _____ Zip Code _____ . Unit N ___ __ __

Development Name _____ No __ Bedrooms ___ __ __

I. **Description of Parties and Premises:** The Housing Authority of the City of Tampa, Florida (hereinafter called Management) does

hereby lease to _____ (herein after called the Tenant) the dwelling

unit described above for the term beginning _____ 19____ and ending at midnight _____ ___ 19___

for a rental of $ _____ for said term

II. **Members of Household:** It is expressly understood and mutually agreed by the parties hereto that only the following named family members will reside in the described dwelling unit: _____

_____

_____

III. **Lease Renewal:** This lease shall be renewed automatically for successive terms of one (1) month at a rental of $ _____ per month, due and payable in advance of the first (1st) day of each calendar month. This rent will remain in effect unless adjusted in accordance with Section VI hereof.

IV. **Security Deposit:** Tenant agrees to pay as a security deposit the amount of $ _____ which is equal to (1) month s rent or $100.00, whichever is greater except that in no event shall the security deposit of an elderly tenant without minor children exceed $100.00. Security deposit shall be paid by money order in full upon admission or a minimum of $100 00 and the balance in equal payments on the first (1st) day of each month for a period not to exceed (6) months.
Security deposit is to be used by Management toward payment of charges for rent, services and charges for damage to the premises owed by Tenant at time of vacating. After deduction of said charges, balance of security deposit will be refunded to the Tenant.

V. **Equipment and Utilities:** Management agrees to furnish a refrigerator, range and space heater for the dwelling unit. In developments where utilities are billed directly to the Authority, Management also agrees to furnish electricity for lighting and food refrigeration; gas or electricity for heating and cooking. Said utilities will be furnished in accordance with Schedule of Allowances. Failure to pay excess utility charges when due will constitute a violation of this lease. If the dwelling unit is not metered so as to determine excess utility consumption, Tenant agrees to pay a reasonable charge for use of an air conditioner, clothes dryer, food freezer or an extra refrigerator. Management will not be responsible for failure to furnish utilities by reason of any cause beyond control of Management.
In developments wherein utilities are billed directly to Tenant by the utility company, the tenant has sole responsibility for securing such service and making prompt payment to maintain uninterrupted services
Charges assessed for excess utilities or charges to Tenant under Section VIII-K shall be due and payable on the first (1st) day of the second (2nd) month following the month in which the charge was incurred.

VI. **Determination of Rent, Dwelling Size, and Eligibility:** As requested by Management, Tenant agrees to furnish accurate information as to family income, employment, and family composition for use by Management in determining whether the rental should be changed, whether the dwelling is still appropriate for Tenants' need and whether Tenant is still eligible for low-rent housing This determination shall be made annually in accordance with the approved Schedule of Rents and Statement of Income and Occupancy Limits posted in the Development Office and Management Central Office.

A. Rents are fixed in Section III hereof, or as adjusted pursuant to the foregoing, will remain in effect for the period between regular rent redeterminations unless there is a change in family composition or income:
1. All interim decreases in rent shall become effective the first (1st) of the month following that in which the Tenant reported the change except that in the corrections of errors, decreases shall be retroactive to the date of the error
2. Interim increases in rent shall become effective the first (1st) of the second (2nd) month following that in which the change occurred.
3. All changes affecting family income, employment and family composition shall be reported at least ten (10) days prior to the first (1st) day of the month in order to facilitate the schedules listed in the items one (1) and two (2) above
4. If, however, it is found that the Tenant has misrepresented to Management the facts upon which his rent is based so that the rent he is paying is less than he should be charged, then the increased rent shall be retroactive to the appropriate date
5. Failure to report income change and/or family composition, can be just cause for eviction and/or retroactive rent

VII. **Management's Obligations:** Management's obligations under this lease shall include the following
A. To maintain the premises and development in decent, safe and sanitary condition;
B. To comply with applicable building codes, housing codes and HUD regulations materially affecting health and safety.
C. To make necessary repairs to the premises and to keep development building and common areas (not otherwise assigned to the tenant for maintenance and upkeep) in a clean and safe condition;
D. To maintain in good and working order the electrical, plumbing, sanitary, heating, ventilating and other facilities supplied, or required to be supplied, by management.
E. To be responsible for collection and disposition of garbage, waste, rubbish and other waste removed from the premises by the Tenant in accordance with section VIII-H hereof.
F. To supply running water to premises and reasonable amounts of hot water and reasonable amounts of heat at appropriate times of the year (according to local custom and usage) except where heat or hot water is generated by an installation within the exclusive control of Tenant;
G. Management is not responsible for loss, damage or injury to tenant or to Tenant's personal property, not the fault of the Housing Authority or its agents.

VIII. **Tenant's Obligations:** The Tenant's obligations under this lease shall include the following
A. To pay rent, excess utilities, maintenance and other charges promptly when due and if not paid by the 5th working day of the month, the Tenant agrees to pay a ten dollar ($10) late charge.
B. Not to assign this lease or to sublet the premises;
C. To not provide accommodations for boarders or lodgers.
D. To use the premises solely as a private dwelling for the Tenant and the Tenant's household as identified in this lease and not to use or permit its use for any other purposes;
E. To abide by necessary and reasonable regulations promulgated by Management for the benefit and well-being of the housing development and the tenants, and which are posted in the development office and incorporated in this lease by reference.
F. To comply with all obligations imposed upon tenants by applicable provisions of building and housing codes materially affect health and safety;
G. To keep the premises and the grounds adjacent thereto in a clean, safe condition and of presentable appearance
H. To dispose of all garbage, rubbish and other waste from the premises in a safe, sanitary manner in accordance with Management regulations;
I. To use only in a reasonable manner all electrical, plumbing, sanitary, heating, ventilating and other facilities and appurtenances, including elevators;
J. To refrain from and to cause his household and guests to refrain from destroying, defacing, damaging or removing any part of the premises or development;
K. To pay reasonable charges (other than normal wear and tear) for the repairs of damages to the premises, development building, facilities, or common areas caused by Tenant, his household or guests (said charges shall be assessed in accordance with guideline "Charges for residents" posted in the development office. Failure to pay said charges when due will constitute a violation of the terms of this lease.
L. To conduct himself and cause other persons on the premises to conduct themselves in a manner which will not disturb his neighbors' peaceful enjoyment of their accommodations and will be conducive to maintaining the development in a decent, safe and sanitary condition;
M. To refrain from illegal or other activity which impairs the physical or social environment of the development.
N. Not to keep an animal of any kind in about or on the premises at any time, except in developments and development areas...

O. To refrain from, and to cause his household and guests to refrain from, parking vehicles in any area other than parking areas designated by Management;

P. Tenant agrees to notify Management promptly of any hazardous defects or deficiencies;

Q. Tenant agrees not to install any additional locks on the exterior doors without making keys available to management.

IX. Hazardous Defects: In the event that the premises are damaged to the extend that conditions are created which are hazadous to life, health or safety of the Tenants.

A. The Tenant shall immediately notify Development Management of the damage;

B. Management shall be responsible for repair of the unit within a reasonable time;

C. Where necessary repairs cannot be made in a reasonable time, Management shall offer standard, alternative accommodations if available;

D. In the event repairs are not made in accordance with B. or alternative accommodations as provided in C. above, abatement of the tenant's rent will be made in proportion to the seriousness of the damage and the loss in value of the unit as a dwelling except that no abatement of rent shall occur if the Tenant rejects the alternative accommodation or if the damages were caused by the Tenant, Tenant's household, or guests.

X. Physical Inspection of Premises: The Tenant or his representative shall be obligated to inspect the premises prior to occupancy. Management will furnish the Tenant with a written statement of the conditions of the premises and equipment provided with the unit. The statement shall be signed by management and tenant, and a copy of the statement shall be retained in the tenant's folder. Management shall be further obligated to inspect, with Tenant, the unit at the time the Tenant vacates and to furnish the tenant with a statement of any charges to be made. In the event the Tenant vacates the unit without proper notice to management, as provided in Section XIV-A, Management's obligation shall be limited to inspection of the unit and posting of resulting charges to Tenant's account.

XI. Right to Entry of Premises: Circumstances under which Management may enter the premises during Tenant's possession thereof shall include but not be limited to:

A. Upon reasonable advance notification to the Tenant, Management shall be permitted to enter the dwelling unit during reasonable hours for the purpose of performing routine inspections and maintenance; for making improvements or repairs, or to show the premises for releasing. A written notice specifying the purpose of management's entry delivered to the premises at least forty-eight (48) hours prior to such entry shall be considered reasonable advance notice

B. Management may enter the premises at any time without advance notification when there is reasonable cause to believe an emergency exists.

C. In the event that the Tenant and all adult members of his household are absent at the time of entry, Management shall leave on the premises a written statement indicating date, time and purpose of said entry.

D. A request from the Tenant for Management to effect repairs within the premises shall be deemed to be consent to enter unless Tenant informs Management otherwise when making such request.

XII. Tenant's Right to Use and Occupancy: The Tenant shall have the right to exclusive use and occupancy of the leased premises for dwelling purposes only, which shall include reasonable accommodation of Tenant's guests or visitors and, with the written consent of management, may incude care of foster children and live-in care of a member of the Tenant's family. (Reasonable accommodations is considered to be ten (10) days in most instances, but is not strictly limited to this)

XIII. Notice Procedures: Procedure to be followed by Management and Tenant in giving notice one to the other under this lease shall require that:

A. Except as provided in Section XI hereof, Notice to the tenant shall be in writing and delivered to the Tenant or to an adult member of the Tenant's household residing in the dwelling or sent by prepaid first class mail properly addressed to Tenant, and

B. Notice to Management shall be in writing delivered to the Development office or Central office or sent by prepaid first class mail properly addressed.

XIV. Termination of Lease:

A. This lease may be terminated by Tenant at any time by giving fifteen (15) days's written notice in the manner specified in Section XIII.

B. This lease may be terminated by Management for good cause by complying with and in accordance with Chapter 83, Part II, Florida Statutes, and successors thereto and this lease as hereinafter described.

1. Good cause as used in this section means serious or repeated violation of the material terms of the lease including, but not limited to, the failure to make payments due under the lease or failure to fulfill Tenant obligations set forth in the lease or having two suits for non-payment of rent filed on the Tenant during a 12-month period.

2. Termination of the lease shall be as follows:

a. Management shall give fourteen (14) days' written notice of termination if said termination is caused by Tenant's failure to pay rent.

b. Management shall give reasonable written notice of termination if the circumstances of the situation create or maintain a threat to the health or safety of other tenants or employees of management.

c. Management shall give thirty (30) days' written notice of termination in all other cases.

Said notice by either party as to termination of this lease shall be given on any day of the month. Said notice shall state reason for termination, shall inform tenant of his right to make such reply as he may wish and of his right to request a hearing in accordance with the Grievance Procedure.

XV. Grievance Procedure: Any dispute or grievance hereunder between the Management and the Tenant shall be settled in accorance with the Grievance Procedure which shall be posted in the development office and is made a part by reference.

XVI. Abandonment of Property: It is understood and agreed by the parties hereto that if for any reason the resident vacates the dwelling unit and furniture and/or personal property is abandoned in the unit, Management will not be liable for the storage and safekeeping of same.

XVII. Included by Reference: It is understood and agreed by the parties hereto that the following shall be incorporated into this lease by reference:

A. Such necessary and reasonable regulations as may presently exist or may be promulgated by Management with the approval of HUD for the benefit and well-being of residents.

B. Adjustment of rents made in accordance with Section VI herein.

Except as provided in Section XVII above no changes herein shall be made except in writing, dated and signed by both parties hereto.

In witness whereof, the parties hereto have executed this lease agreement this _____ day of _____, 19_____ at Tampa, Florida.

THE HOUSING AUTHORITY OF THE CITY OF TAMPA, FLORIDA

By: _____

Title: _____

Executed in the presence of:

_____   _____
                                        Signature of Resident

_____   _____
                                        Signature of Resident

North East Multi-Regional
Training, Inc.

1 Smoke Tree Plaza, Suite 111
North Aurora, IL 60542

Account No. _____

THE HOUSING AUTHORITY OF THE CITY OF ATLANTA, GEORGIA

DWELLING LEASE

Section 1 — DESCRIPTION OF PARTIES AND PREMISES

1. Date of Lease	2. Management (Lessor) Atlanta Housing Authority		3. Lessee (Name of Tenant)		
4. Address	5. Dwelling #	6. Housing Project		7. No. of Bedrooms	8. Floor(s)
9. Initial Total Tenant payment (pro rata rent) $	10. Total Tenant Payment (rent) $	11. Term To Commence		12. Term To End	
13. Security Deposit (Total) $	14. Initial Payment Security Deposit $				
15. Anniversary Date	16. Utilities Furnished (Check) Quantities as Posted in Management Office				
	Heat	Hot Water	Cold Water	Electricity	Gas

MEMBERS OF HOUSEHOLD WHO WILL RESIDE IN UNIT

1.	8.
2.	9.
3.	10.
4.	11.
5.	12.
6.	13.
7.	14.

In consideration of the mutual agreements and covenants set forth below (the same being fully included as part of this Lease) Management hereby leases to Tenant and Tenant hereby leases from Management for a private dwelling the unit designated above, together with fixtures and equipment belonging thereto. Parties to this lease listed above as Management and Tenant are hereinafter referred to as "Management" and "Tenant".

TENANT	ATLANTA HOUSING AUTHORITY
Head of Household _____	
Spouse _____	By _____ Housing Manager

SECTION II — COVENANTS AND AGREEMENTS OF THE PARTIES

RENEWAL OF TENANCY
1. After the original term specified in Section I herein, this lease shall automatically be renewed for successive terms of one calendar month, until terminated pursuant to Section II, paragraph 15 hereof.

REQUIRED PAYMENTS
2. The term "Required Payments" shall include (a) the amount fixed as rent for use and occupancy of the premises, including provision of services and equipment (range and refrigerator) furnished by management without extra costs; (b) amounts chargeable for excess consumption of utilities, additional or special services, and use of special equipment; and (c) reasonable charges for maintenance and repair beyond normal wear and tear to the leased dwelling, project buildings, project facilities or other project areas, caused by the Tenant, by members of the Tenant's family, or by their guests. A schedule of repair charges shall be posted in the Project Management Office.

PAYMENTS DUE UNDER LEASE
3. The basic rental for the original term of this lease and for each renewal term of one calendar month shall be the amounts shown in Section I herein. This rent will remain in effect unless adjusted in accordance with the provisions of Section II, Paragraph 6 hereof. Required payments shall be due and payable monthly in advance on the first day of each calendar month and shall be considered delinquent after the fifth or next business day of each month except that charges assessed under Section II, paragraph 2(b)(c), shall become due the first calendar day of the second month following the month in which the charge was made and shall be considered delinquent after the fifth or next business day of that month. All payments due hereunder shall be paid at the Project Management Office by check or money order. For all checks returned to the Authority for insufficient funds, a ten dollar ($10.00) return check fee shall be charged to the Tenant's account. Once a check is returned, the Tenant shall be required to make all payments with a money order or cashiers check.

SECURITY DEPOSIT
4. Tenant agrees to pay a security deposit as provided in Section I herein to be used by Management at the termination of this lease toward reimbursement of the charges for maintenance beyond normal wear and tear to the dwelling unit caused by Tenant, his/her family, or dependents who are members of the household or Tenant's guests and any rent or charges for court costs and excess utilities owed by Tenant. Payment of the security deposit is to be as stated in Section I above. Management agrees to return the security deposit, without interest, to Tenant when he/she vacates, less any deductions for any of the charges indicated above. Management shall give Tenant a written statement of any such charges for damages or other charges to be deducted from the security deposit or both. The security deposit may not be used to pay rent or other charges while the Tenant occupies the dwelling unit.

UTILITIES
5. Management agrees to furnish to Tenant without extra charge utilities for use on the premises of the types and quantity not to exceed the authorized amounts provided in the Schedule of Utility Allowance posted in the Project Management Office and incorporated herein by reference. Utilities consumed in excess of the authorized amount shall be charged to the Tenant's account as an additional required payment.

REDETERMINATION OF RENT, DWELLING SIZE, ELIGIBILITY
6. Once each year as requested by Management, Tenant agrees to provide accurate information to Management as to total family income, employment, and composition, for use by Management in determining whether the rent amount should be changed, whether the dwelling size is still appropriate for Tenant's needs, and whether Tenant is still eligible for low-rent housing. This determination will be made in accordance with the approved regulations establishing Admission and Continued Occupancy Policies for Management, the maximum income limits for Admission and Continued Occupancy, and the Schedule of Rents then in effect and available in the Project Management Office. The review to determine the Tenant's current eligibility and rental shall be effective on the Tenant's anniversary date as specified in Section I above, or as otherwise provided in the rules and regulations of Management: (a) Rent as fixed in Section I hereof or as adjusted pursuant to the above will remain in effect for the period between regular rent determinations unless during such period: (i) Tenant can show a decline in income which would result in his/her payment of rent in excess of 30% of his/she income; provided, however, decline in income is subsequent to such an interim rent adjustment and prior to the next anniversary date, the Tenant's income increases, the Tenant shall report such increase and his/her rent shall be adjusted accordingly: (ii) Tenant commences to receive public assistance or his/her public assistance is terminated. Such a change must be reported to Management within (10) days of its occurrence. (iii) it is found that Tenant has misrepresented to Management the facts upon which his rent is based, so that the rent he/her is paying is less than he/she should have been charged, then the increase in rent will be made retroactive to the date that the increase would have taken effect. In the event of any rent adjustment pursuant to the above, Management will deliver a "Notice of Rent Adjustment" to Tenant by personal service or regular mail. In the case of rent increases, the adjustment will become effective and the increased rent will become due on the first day of the second following month. (a) In the case where rent is zero and the rent increases, the adjustment will become effective and the increase rent will become effective on the first day of the month following that in which the Tenant reports the change. In the case of rent decreases the adjustment will become effective on the first of the month following that in which the Tenant reports the change. (b) If Management determines that the size of the dwelling unit is no longer appropriate to Tenant's needs, Management may amend this lease by notice to Tenant, by personal service or regular mail, that Tenant shall be required to move to another unit within the project in which he/she lives, giving Tenant a reasonable time in which to move. (c) If Management finds that Tenant's income has increased so that it is above the approved income limits for continuing occupancy in low-rent housing, Management shall then determine whether or not Tenant can, with reasonable effort, find other suitable housing. (1) If Management determines that due to special circumstances, Tenant will be unable to find other suitable housing, Tenant may remain in low-rent housing so long as the special circumstances exist,

North East Multi-Regional
Training, Inc.
1 Smoke Tree Plaza, Suite 111
North Aurora, IL 60542